Title Page

The Disappeared

The Complete 360° Blueprint for Finding a Missing Person

From the First Hour to the Final Answer

Fazal Abubakkar Esaf

A definitive guide for families, investigators, law enforcement professionals, journalists, and search specialists.

Table of Contents

"The most painful state is not knowing—because hope refuses to die,and certainty never arrives."

Copyright Page

First Edition — 2026

Dedication

To those who wait.

To the mothers who still listen for a door that never opened.

To the fathers who replay the last conversation.

To the siblings who refuse to stop searching.

To the friends who keep a number saved, hoping it will someday ring again.

And to those who vanished—

You are not forgotten.

You are still being searched for.

Epigraph

"The most painful state is not knowing—
because hope refuses to die,
and certainty never arrives."

Acknowledgments

This book exists because of the quiet courage of families who endure the most difficult uncertainty of all: not knowing where someone they love has gone.

Across the world, investigators, volunteers, journalists, search teams, and law enforcement officers enter demanding terrain—both physical and emotional—driven by a single purpose: to bring someone home, or at the very least, to bring truth.

Their discipline shaped the operational thinking behind this work.

Their persistence inspired its depth.

I also acknowledge the psychologists, behavioral analysts, forensic experts, and search strategists whose collective knowledge has transformed missing-person investigations from reactive efforts into structured, intelligence-driven operations.

Most importantly, this book is written for ordinary people forced into extraordinary circumstances—individuals who never expected to learn the language of investigations, yet suddenly must think and act like professionals.

May this guide provide clarity when chaos strikes, direction when time is slipping away, and strength when hope feels fragile.

— Fazal Abubakkar Esaf

Preface

Someone disappears every few seconds somewhere in the world.

Most people believe it is something that happens to others—in distant cities, unfamiliar neighborhoods, or headlines briefly noticed and quickly forgotten.

Until one day, absence enters their own life.

And nothing is ever the same again.

When a person vanishes, confusion becomes the first enemy. Families freeze. Friends panic. Critical hours dissolve into unstructured action. Evidence is unknowingly compromised. Opportunities are missed.

Not because people do not care—

but because no one ever trained them for this moment.

This book was written to change that.

The Disappeared is not a collection of theories. It is a structured operational manual designed to transform fear into focused action.

Within these pages, you will not be told merely to "stay strong" or "wait for updates." You will learn what to do, when to do it, and why it matters. You will learn how professionals think.

Because when time is critical, clarity saves lives.

Introduction

When the Unthinkable Becomes Reality

There is a moment—quiet, almost ordinary—when realization begins.

A phone call goes unanswered.

A message remains unread.

A routine arrival never happens.

At first, the mind searches for harmless explanations: traffic, a dead battery, a forgotten charger.

But as hours pass, unease hardens into fear.

Then comes the question that changes everything:

What if something is wrong?

Most missing-person cases are not solved by luck. They are solved through speed, structure, behavioral insight, and intelligent coordination.

Yet families are rarely prepared.

Many unknowingly:

- Overwrite or lose digital evidence
- Delay reporting critical information
- Misinterpret behavioral warning signs
- Scatter search efforts without coordination
- Trust unreliable or misleading leads
- Exhaust time and energy in the wrong direction

Meanwhile, time—the single most valuable investigative asset—continues to move, whether action is taken or not.

This book exists to ensure that when the unthinkable happens, action replaces paralysis, structure replaces chaos, and informed decisions replace costly mistakes.

1. When Absence Becomes an Emergency

Introduction: The Moment That Changes Everything

Disappearance does not begin with certainty.

It begins with doubt.

A delay feels ordinary—until it does not. A routine interruption quietly shifts into something else: unease, then concern, then a creeping recognition that the familiar logic governing a person's movements no longer applies. Most families lose irreplaceable time not because they failed to care, but because they failed to recognize the precise moment when delay becomes danger.

This chapter exists to eliminate that hesitation.

Absence is not always an emergency. People arrive late, batteries die, plans change, and schedules fracture. Everyday life contains countless benign explanations for temporary silence. But every emergency begins as absence. The earliest phase of a missing-person incident is indistinguishable, at first glance, from normal delay. The professional skill—whether exercised by families, caregivers, administrators, or first responders—is knowing how to tell the difference.

Disappearance is not defined by drama or duration. It is defined by broken patterns, emerging risk signals, and the sudden loss of predictability. Once that threshold is crossed, the search has already begun—whether anyone has acknowledged it or not.

This chapter establishes a disciplined framework for recognizing that threshold, acting decisively, and avoiding the most common cognitive and procedural errors that cost time, evidence, and lives.

1. Missing vs. Delayed — The Critical Distinction

The single most important judgment in the early phase of a disappearance is whether a person is delayed or missing. This determination governs every subsequent action: whether to wait, whom to notify, what to preserve, and how urgently to mobilize resources.

1.1 The Delayed Person

A delayed person is an individual whose absence remains consistent with their established behavior, routine, and context, and whose delay has a plausible, verifiable explanation. The key elements are consistency *and* verifiability.

Common examples include:

- Transportation disruptions with confirmation (flight delays, public transit outages, traffic accidents reported on known routes)
- Known schedule changes that were communicated in advance
- Predictable communication gaps (work shifts, travel through low-signal areas, religious observances)
- Established patterns of late return that have occurred repeatedly without adverse outcomes

A delay may still provoke concern. Concern alone, however, does not justify emergency mobilization. In delayed scenarios, the person's behavior remains logical when evaluated against their personal history and current circumstances. The timeline may be inconvenient or stressful, but it does not yet indicate elevated risk.

1.2 The Missing Person

A person becomes missing when their absence breaks pattern, logic, or safety expectations and cannot be reasonably explained within context. This determination is behavioral, not chronological.

An individual should be considered missing when one or more of the following conditions are present:

- Communication stops abruptly and unusually, especially mid-conversation or during an expected check-in
- Plans are broken without notice in ways that contradict prior reliability
- Personal belongings critical for survival or mobility are left behind (wallet, phone, keys, medication)
- The individual fails to arrive at a known destination without explanation
- Behavior prior to disappearance suggests risk, distress, coercion, or impairment

It is essential to emphasize a foundational reality:

There is no legally required waiting period to report a missing person.

The widely believed requirement to wait 24 or 48 hours is a dangerous myth. In most jurisdictions, missing-person reports can be filed immediately when circumstances justify concern. Law enforcement agencies and search professionals consistently affirm that early reporting improves outcomes and does not penalize families for acting promptly.

The distinction between delayed and missing is not about optimism versus alarmism. It is about evidence-based judgment.

2. Statistical Survival Timelines — What Time Actually Means

Time behaves differently in missing-person cases. It is not linear. It is decisive.

While no timeline guarantees outcomes, decades of investigative data reveal consistent patterns in recovery probability and case complexity. Understanding these patterns helps families and professionals resist the false comfort of waiting.

2.1 General Survival Realities (Not Guarantees)

Across a broad range of cases, the following trends are observed:

- **First 6 hours:** Highest probability of safe recovery
- **First 24 hours:** Maximum intervention impact
- **After 72 hours:** Recovery probability begins declining sharply
- **After 7 days:** Case complexity increases exponentially

These benchmarks are descriptive, not predictive. Individual outcomes vary widely based on age, environment, health, and circumstances. However, the overarching trend is unmistakable: early action preserves options; delay eliminates them.

2.2 High-Risk Populations

Certain categories of missing persons follow significantly shorter survival curves and require immediate escalation:

- Children and adolescents
- Individuals with cognitive impairment or developmental disabilities
- People experiencing mental health crises

- Those with medical dependencies (insulin, cardiac medication, mobility aids)
- Situations involving suspected abduction, domestic violence, or human trafficking

In these cases, hours—or even minutes—can determine survivability. Waiting for certainty in high-risk scenarios is equivalent to accepting preventable harm.

2.3 The Professional Truth

Professionals understand a difficult but necessary truth:

Speed does not guarantee success—but delay guarantees disadvantage.

Rapid response preserves evidence, memories, locations, and digital traces. Once lost, these elements cannot be reconstructed. Time does not merely pass; it actively erodes investigative leverage.

3. The "First 24 Hours" Myth — Why It Misleads Families

Popular culture, true-crime media, and dramatized investigations often repeat the phrase: "The first 24 hours are critical." While technically accurate, this framing is incomplete—and often harmful.

3.1 What Professionals Actually Know

In practice, the first **60 to 120 minutes** after recognition often matter more than the next 23 hours combined. This is the window when:

- Witnesses are still present and unprompted
- Surveillance footage has not been overwritten
- Digital location data remains intact
- Environmental evidence is uncontaminated

- The missing person's trail is warm enough to follow

By contrast, waiting to act until a symbolic 24-hour mark often means that decisive opportunities have already expired.

3.2 Why the Myth Persists

The "24-hour rule" persists because it offers emotional permission to wait. It externalizes responsibility to the clock instead of the evidence. For families in shock, this delay can feel safer than acting on uncertainty.

3.3 The Hidden Costs of Waiting

Waiting introduces specific, measurable harms:

- Evidence is deleted, overwritten, or altered
- Physical locations are cleaned, repurposed, or weather-exposed
- Witness memory degrades rapidly within hours
- Digital systems auto-update, sync, or expire logs
- Narratives solidify around assumptions rather than facts

3.4 The Real Rule

Act the moment behavior deviates from safety logic—not the moment the clock allows you to.

Time thresholds are administrative conveniences. Risk thresholds save lives.

4. Immediate Cognitive Traps Families Fall Into

When disappearance occurs, the human brain enters survival mode. Stress hormones spike, attention narrows, and decision-making becomes distorted. These reactions are normal—but they are also dangerous.

Understanding common cognitive traps allows families and professionals to override instinct with structured judgment.

Trap 1: Normalcy Bias

"This has happened before. They always come back."

Reality: Past delays do not predict current safety. Each incident must be evaluated on its own conditions. Normalcy bias causes people to underestimate new threats by over-relying on familiar outcomes.

Trap 2: Self-Blame Paralysis

"If I report too early, I'll look foolish or over reactive."

Reality: Early reporting saves lives. Law enforcement and search professionals overwhelmingly prefer false alarms to late cases. No penalty exists for acting in good faith.

Trap 3: Over-Rationalization

"They must be busy. The phone is probably off."

Reality: Disappearance rarely presents as a single dramatic anomaly. It emerges through clusters of small, compounding inconsistencies that are easy to dismiss individually.

Trap 4: Emotional Freeze

Families often wait for certainty before acting.

Reality: Certainty usually arrives too late. Professional response is designed to function under uncertainty; waiting for clarity defeats the purpose of early intervention.

5. Rapid Response Checklist — First Recognition Phase

The moment concern becomes justified, action must shift from speculation to preservation. The following checklist is designed for immediate use within the first hour of recognition.

5.1 Immediate Actions (Within the First Hour)

- Record the exact last confirmed contact time
- Preserve all digital devices (do not reset, unlock, or charge unnecessarily)
- Document, in writing:
    - Last known location
    - Clothing worn
    - Emotional state during last contact
    - Recent conflicts, stressors, or unusual behavior
- Secure the living space and any last-seen location
- Halt speculative conversations that distort memory and contaminate recall

5.2 Do Not

- Delete messages, call logs, or app data
- Repeatedly call or ping the phone (this can overwrite location and battery data)
- Clean rooms, vehicles, or personal spaces
- Spread unverified theories or assumptions

Preservation is as important as pursuit. Once altered, original conditions cannot be restored.

6. Behavioral Red-Flag Assessment

When emotions blur judgment, structured assessment restores clarity. The following behavioral indicators help translate instinct into defensible risk evaluation.

Red Flag	Risk Level
Abrupt silence without explanation	High
Personal items left behind (wallet, phone, medication)	Critical
Uncharacteristic route or behavior	High
Recent emotional distress or instability	High
Financial or legal pressure	Medium–High
Threats, stalking, or active disputes	Critical
Missed essential obligation (work, school, caregiving)	High
Sudden identity, appearance, or digital changes	Critical

Interpretive Rule: Multiple medium-risk indicators equal one high-risk event. Risk compounds; it does not average out.

7. Professional Insight: How Investigators Think

Investigators are not looking for drama. They are looking for pattern disruption.

They assess:

- What should have happened next
- What usually happens in similar circumstances
- What did not happen—and why that absence matters

Intuition is valuable, but it must be translated into structured justification. Statements such as *"something feels wrong"* become actionable when paired with observable deviations: missed check-ins, broken routines, unexplained silence, or abandoned necessities.

The moment you can clearly articulate *why* someone is missing—using behavior, context, and risk signals—is the moment professionals can act decisively.

Key Principle to Carry Forward

Disappearance is not defined by time.

It is defined by broken patterns, emerging risk, and the sudden loss of predictability.

Once that threshold is crossed, the search has already begun—whether anyone has acknowledged it or not. The purpose of this chapter is to ensure that recognition happens early, clearly, and without hesitation.

2. The Golden Hour Protocol

How the First 60 Minutes Can Shape the Entire Investigation

When a person vanishes, time does not simply pass.

It erases, overwrites, and scatters.

Witnesses forget. Cameras record over footage. Phones sync, update, and alter metadata. Locations change as people move through them. Weather alters terrain, footprints, and scent. Digital trails grow cold or distort themselves through automated systems.

The earliest phase of a disappearance is not merely important—it is structurally decisive. This is the window in which reality is still intact. Once it closes, investigators are forced to work with fragments, reconstructions, and assumptions.

Experienced investigators often say:

"Show me what happened in the first hour, and I will tell you how solvable the case is."

The Golden Hour is not about panic-driven speed. It is about calm, controlled precision. It is about behaving deliberately under pressure, even without formal training.

You do not need to be a professional.

You need to behave like one.

1. What Is the Golden Hour?

The Golden Hour begins the moment you recognize a critical truth:

This absence is not normal.

Not when police arrive. Not when a report is filed. Not when others agree something is wrong.

The clock starts with recognition.

Most families unknowingly lose this hour to frantic calling, scattered conversations, emotional escalation, and unstructured searching. These reactions are understandable—but they are costly. While attention disperses, critical evidence quietly degrades.

The objective of the Golden Hour is not to solve the case. It is to prevent irreversible loss.

Your priorities are simple and sequential:

1. Stabilize
2. Preserve
3. Document
4. Escalate

In that order.

Skipping steps or reversing this sequence increases confusion and weakens every action that follows.

2. Minute-by-Minute Action Plan

This framework exists to prevent cognitive overload and convert fear into executable steps. You do not need to complete everything perfectly. You need to complete the right things deliberately.

Minute 0–5 — Confirm the Anomaly

Do not assume. Verify.

Ask objective questions:

- Was there a scheduled arrival or check-in?
- Was the route or destination predictable?
- Is the silence unusual for this person?
- Are they unreachable across multiple channels?

If the behavior breaks pattern—even slightly—activate the protocol immediately. Do not wait for certainty. Certainty is retrospective; safety is not.

Minute 5–10 — Anchor the Timeline

Write everything down physically. Do not rely on memory, screenshots, or mental reconstruction.

Record:

- Last confirmed contact
- Exact time and date
- Method (call, text, in-person)
- Emotional tone
- Stated destination or plan
- Expected arrival or return time

Timelines are the spine of investigations. Without them, cases bend toward speculation. Memory begins distorting within hours; written documentation preserves original truth.

Minute 10–15 — Identify Immediate Risk

Ask three professional-grade questions:

1. **Medical vulnerability:** Does the person rely on medication, mobility aids, or regular care?
2. **Emotional state:** Were there signs of distress, instability, fear, or withdrawal?
3. **External threat:** Is there any reason someone might wish to harm, coerce, or intercept them?

If the answer to any question is yes, elevate the situation immediately. Do not minimize risk to avoid alarm. Early escalation protects credibility; late escalation erodes it.

Minute 15–25 — Call Strategically (Not Emotionally)

Most people call everyone.

Professionals call the right people, in the right order, with the right questions.

Priority contact order:

- The last person who saw them
- The destination they were heading toward
- Household members
- Close friends
- Workplace or school
- Transportation providers, if relevant

Ask precise, neutral questions:

- "What exact time did you last see them?"
- "Did anything unusual occur?"
- "Were they alone?"
- "Which direction did they go?"

Avoid leading questions such as "Did they seem upset?" Leading questions contaminate memory and reduce evidentiary value.

3. Evidence Preservation — The Highest Priority

Families frequently destroy evidence while trying to help. Preservation is not passivity—it is protection.

Treat the environment as if investigators are already present.

Preserve Immediately:

- Bedroom or living space
- Vehicle
- Desk or work area
- Digital devices
- Written notes or documents
- Trash bins
- Doors, windows, and entry points

Do Not:

- Clean or reorganize
- Wash clothing or bedding
- Charge devices unnecessarily
- Allow visitors to walk through the space

Every footprint, fingerprint, and moved object adds noise to the investigative signal. Noise hides patterns. Patterns solve cases.

You are not being dramatic. You are protecting truth.

4. Securing Digital Devices — The Silent Witnesses

Phones, laptops, and tablets often contain more reliable information than human recollection. They preserve movement, intention, and behavior without emotion.

These devices may contain:

- Location history
- Communication records
- Search activity
- Passwords and access points

- Transportation data

Golden Rules:

- Place devices in a secure location
- Keep them powered as found
- Disable auto-lock only if already unlocked
- Photograph screens if critical information is visible

Never:

- Guess passwords repeatedly
- Reset or factory-wipe devices
- Install tracking or forensic software
- "Search through everything" in panic

Digital curiosity can permanently destroy forensic value. If the primary phone is missing, document that fact immediately—it materially changes the risk assessment.

5. Protecting the Last Known Point (LKP)

The Last Known Point is the geographic heartbeat of the investigation. Once altered, it cannot be restored.

Control the Space

Limit access to one or two trusted individuals. Avoid group searches, emotional gatherings, or well-meaning helpers in the immediate area. Activity obscures evidence.

If the disappearance occurred in a public location, document immediately:

- Lighting conditions

- Visible cameras
- Open businesses
- Transit stops
- Potential witnesses

Small observations made early often become decisive pivots later.

6. Escalation — When to Contact Law Enforcement

Contact law enforcement immediately if:

- The missing person is a child
- There is medical dependency
- Mental health risk is present
- Violence or coercion is possible
- The disappearance is entirely out of character

Otherwise, trust your judgment. You are not required to wait. Early reporting is interpreted as responsible, not irrational.

When contacting authorities, provide facts—not theories. Professionals build cases on clarity, not speculation.

7. Emotional Discipline during the Golden Hour

Fear spreads faster than information. One person must become the calm center.

Not emotionless. Not detached. But operational.

If possible, assign roles:

- One person documents
- One person makes calls

- One person secures locations

Structure reduces panic. Panic destroys precision.

The Golden Hour Template (Operational Use)

Missing Person Identification

- Name:
- Age:
- Physical Description:

Timeline Anchor

- Last Seen By:
- Location:
- Date:
- Time:
- Last Contact Method:
    - Call / Text / In Person / Other
- Emotional State Observed:
- Intended Destination:

Immediate Risk Scan

- Medical Condition: Yes / No
- Mental Health Concern: Yes / No
- Recent Distress: Yes / No
- Threat History: Yes / No
- Risk Level: Low / Elevated / High / Critical

Evidence Secured

- Bedroom
- Vehicle
- Phone
- Laptop
- Notes
- Nearby cameras identified

Primary Contacts Logged

- Name
- Relationship
- Time Contacted
- Key Information

Law Enforcement

- Contacted: Yes / No
- Agency:
- Officer Name:
- Report Number:

Principle to Remember

The Golden Hour is not about finding the person immediately.

It is about preventing the truth from disappearing before investigators can see it.

What you protect now may become the detail that breaks the case open later.

You have stabilized the moment.

Next comes the harder question:

How dangerous is this disappearance—really?

3. Risk Profiling the Missing Person

Not All Disappearances Are Equal

Every disappearance carries risk—but risk is not uniform.

A child who wanders into a park at dusk, a teenager fleeing conflict, an adult intentionally leaving town, or an individual experiencing psychological distress each represent fundamentally different investigative problems. Treating them the same wastes time, misdirects resources, and can place the missing person in greater danger.

Professionals do not ask first *"Where should we search?"* They ask:

"How dangerous is this disappearance, and why?"

The purpose of this chapter is to teach you how to quantify risk before acting, so that urgency, strategy, and resources align with reality—not fear, denial, or guesswork.

1. Why Risk Profiling Matters

Law enforcement does not treat every missing person the same. Search-and-rescue teams, behavioral analysts, and investigators adjust their response based on perceived threat, vulnerability, and intent.

Early risk profiling determines:

- **Urgency:** How fast the case must escalate
- **Methodology:** Which investigative and search techniques are appropriate
- **Resource Allocation:** Who must be notified and in what order
- **Safety Measures:** What precautions are required to protect both the missing person and searchers

Without structured risk assessment, families often exhaust themselves pursuing low-probability explanations—voluntary absence, misunderstandings, benign delays—while evidence decays and high-risk indicators go unaddressed.

Risk profiling does not mean assuming the worst.

It means refusing to assume safety without evidence.

2. Building a Threat Matrix

A Threat Matrix is a professional tool used to categorize disappearances based on vulnerability, intent, and external danger. It replaces emotional reasoning with comparative analysis.

Each category below reflects distinct risk dynamics and requires tailored response priorities.

A. Child (Ages 0–12)

Children represent the highest inherent-risk category in missing-person investigations.

Risk Factors

- Limited physical strength and survival skills
- Incomplete understanding of danger
- Dependence on adults for navigation, food, and shelter
- Increased vulnerability to opportunistic abduction, especially in urban or transit-adjacent areas

Indicators Requiring Immediate Escalation

- Sudden disappearance from home, school, or supervised activity
- Presence of unknown individuals or suspicious vehicles

nearby
- Medical dependency (medication, allergies, assistive devices)

Suggested Action

Maximum priority. Activate Golden Hour protocols immediately. Treat absence as dangerous until proven otherwise.

B. Teen Runaway (Ages 13–17)

Teen disappearances are among the most misunderstood and frequently misclassified.

Risk Factors

- Developmental drive for autonomy
- Peer influence and online relationships
- High emotional volatility
- Exposure to exploitation, trafficking, or coercion

Indicators to Escalate

- Leaving without essentials (phone, money, medication)
- Prior runaway behavior combined with escalating distress
- Involvement in risky online or in-person social circles

Suggested Action

Medium to high priority. Monitor digital footprints, social contacts, and peer networks aggressively. Do not assume safety based on past returns.

C. Adult Voluntary Disappearance (Ages 18+)

Adults possess legal autonomy, complicating early assessments. However, autonomy does not eliminate risk.

Risk Factors

- Financial, legal, or relational stressors
- Desire for identity reinvention or escape
- Shame, fear, or avoidance behaviors

Indicators to Escalate

- Abrupt withdrawal from all contacts
- Liquidation of assets or unexplained financial activity
- Deliberate severing of digital traces

Suggested Action

Variable priority. Evaluate intent versus coercion carefully. Escalate immediately if additional red flags emerge.

D. Mental Health Risk (All Ages)

Psychological vulnerability dramatically shortens survival timelines.

Risk Factors

- Diagnosed psychiatric conditions
- Depression, anxiety, psychosis, or suicidal ideation
- History of self-harm or hospitalization

Indicators to Escalate

- Explicit or implied threats of self-harm
- Neglect of basic needs
- Sudden isolation from support systems

Suggested Action

High risk. Treat as time-critical. Involve mental health professionals and emergency services immediately.

E. Kidnapping or Coercion Probability

This category carries the highest urgency regardless of age.

Risk Factors

- History of stalking, domestic violence, or threats
- Predictable routines or vulnerable locations
- Recent conflicts involving power imbalance

Indicators to Escalate

- Witness reports of suspicious activity
- Evidence of forced entry or struggle
- Abrupt behavioral change immediately prior to disappearance

Suggested Action

Critical priority. Activate law enforcement immediately. Do not attempt independent resolution.

3. Quantifying Risk — A Professional Scoring Tool

To remove emotion from decision-making, professionals often assign numerical values to risk indicators. This approach transforms intuition into defensible action.

Risk Scoring Matrix

Factor	Low (1)	Medium (2)	High (3)
Age Vulnerability	Teen/Adult	Older Teen / Young Adult	Child
Mental Health	None	Mild / Situational	Severe / History of Self-Harm
Circumstances	Voluntary absence likely	Ambiguous	Suspicious / Threat present
Recent Behavior	Normal	Minor deviations	Major warning signs
Environment	Safe / familiar	Moderately risky	High-risk, urban, or isolated

Interpretation

- **5–7:** Monitor closely; limited investigation
- **8–10:** Escalate; notify local authorities
- **11–15:** Immediate full-scale response; Golden Hour protocols fully active

Scoring does not predict outcomes. It prioritizes response.

4. Applying the Threat Matrix in Real Time

1. Gather all available data: age, location, last contact, mental

health history, social connections

2. Assign each factor to the appropriate category
3. Score objectively—do not minimize to avoid fear
4. Determine urgency and deploy resources accordingly

Risk assessment is not a one-time act. Reassess continuously as new information emerges. A medium-risk case can escalate to critical within minutes.

5. Professional Insight

Not all disappearances are emergencies—but all emergencies begin with a wrongly assumed normalcy.

Always document your rationale, even if later deemed unnecessary. Documentation strengthens law enforcement response and preserves your own strategic clarity.

Risk profiling is not about imagining worst-case scenarios.

It is about preparing for them before they become inevitable.

Key Takeaways

- Children and mental health cases demand immediate priority
- Teen cases are high-risk but variable; digital environments matter
- Adult disappearances require intent analysis, not assumptions
- Kidnapping indicators require instant escalation
- Scoring tools convert instinct into structured, defensible response

4. The Last Known Point (LKP) Method

Using Geographic Anchoring to Strategically Locate Missing Persons

Every successful missing-person investigation begins at a single point: the **Last Known Point (LKP)**.

Across jurisdictions worldwide, law enforcement agencies, search-and-rescue (SAR) units, and investigative teams rely on the LKP to structure searches, prioritize resources, and prevent the uncontrolled dispersion of effort. When cases fail, it is often because the LKP was misunderstood, poorly documented, or contaminated before it could be operationalized.

The LKP is not merely a location.

It is the anchor for probability, movement modeling, and decision-making under uncertainty. Properly used, it transforms fear into geometry, chaos into structure, and time into measurable advantage.

This chapter provides professional-grade frameworks, checklists, and templates to apply the LKP method with precision—whether you are a family member, volunteer coordinator, or investigative professional.

1. Understanding the Last Known Point

Definition

The **Last Known Point (LKP)** is the most recent location at which a missing person's presence can be **confirmed** through reliable means:

- Direct visual confirmation
- Digital verification

- Credible, time-specific witness testimony

The emphasis is on *confirmed*. Assumptions, inferences, and unverified sightings do not constitute an LKP.

Core Principles

- The LKP is the **origin of probability mapping**.
- All systematic search efforts must **radiate outward** from this point.
- Multiple LKPs may exist if a person was moving; each must be treated **sequentially**, not blended together.

Each new LKP resets probability. Failing to recognize this leads to expanded searches built on outdated assumptions.

Common Sources of LKP Data

- Witness statements (with exact times and locations)
- CCTV or private surveillance footage
- Mobile phone GPS data or cellular tower records
- Transportation records (bus cards, train entries, tolls)
- ATM or card transactions
- Last verified online activity or geotagged social media posts

Professional Note:

An LKP does not guarantee continued presence. It marks the point of *maximum leverage*. With every passing hour, uncertainty expands outward, and search efficiency declines exponentially.

2. Geographic Anchoring

Geographic anchoring converts the LKP from a dot on a map into a structured search environment.

Step 1: Pinpoint Exact Coordinates

- Confirm the precise address or GPS coordinates
- Record how the location was verified (witness, video, digital)
- Timestamp the confirmation

Approximate locations create approximate searches. Precision at this stage determines everything that follows.

Step 2: Assess Surrounding Terrain

Evaluate the environment within immediate proximity:

- Urban vs. rural setting
- Road density and traffic flow
- Water bodies (rivers, lakes, drainage canals)
- Dense vegetation, forest, or open terrain
- Physical barriers (fences, construction zones, buildings)

Terrain dictates movement speed, concealment, and survivability.

Step 3: Identify Points of Egress

Determine how a person could reasonably leave the area:

- Roads and intersections
- Footpaths, trails, or alleys
- Transit stops or stations
- Informal paths used by pedestrians or animals

These egress points often become directional indicators in later modeling.

Step 4: Map Environmental Risk Zones

Highlight areas that increase danger or likelihood of harm:

- Bodies of water
- Isolated or poorly lit zones
- Known crime hotspots
- Industrial sites or construction areas
- Medical risk locations for vulnerable individuals

Step 5: Document Everything

Maintain an LKP log containing:

- Time-stamped observations
- Witness input
- Environmental notes
- Photographs or sketches when possible

Documentation preserves situational truth as conditions evolve.

3. Movement Radius Modeling

Once the LKP is confirmed, the next task is estimating how far the person could have traveled. This converts uncertainty into probability-based planning.

Key Factors

- **Time elapsed** since disappearance
- **Physical capability** (age, health, injuries)
- **Environmental constraints** (terrain, barriers, weather)

- **Transportation access** (vehicle, transit, bicycle)
- **Behavioral intent** (voluntary travel, panic, evasion, confusion)

Step-by-Step Radius Estimation

Walking Distance Benchmarks

- Average adult: ~5 km per hour
- Children or elderly individuals: ~2–3 km per hour

Adjust downward for rough terrain, obstacles, or physical limitations.

Transportation Expansion

- Identify access to buses, trains, taxis, or personal vehicles
- Document any known or suspected mode of transport

Transportation radically expands radius and must be treated as a separate probability model.

Create Concentric Probability Zones

- **Zone 1:** 0–2 km — highest probability (first hour on foot)
- **Zone 2:** 2–5 km — moderate probability (2–3 hours)
- **Zone 3:** Beyond 5 km — lower probability, expanded after 6–12 hours

These distances are not fixed. They must be adjusted for terrain, weather, and behavioral context.

4. Probability Rings

Probability rings allow teams to focus resources where they are most likely to succeed.

Implementation

1. Mark the LKP as the center point
2. Overlay concentric rings based on movement radius modeling
3. Assign operational priority to each ring

Priority Structure

- **Ring 1:** Immediate search
    - Highest personnel density
    - Canine units, drones, rapid visual sweeps
- **Ring 2:** Secondary search
    - Mobile patrols
    - Neighborhood canvassing
    - Door-to-door inquiries
- **Ring 3:** Tertiary search
    - Road checks
    - Alerts and broader terrain coverage

Professional Tip:

Probability is dynamic. Each ring must be time-stamped and reassessed as hours pass. Static maps create false confidence.

5. Directional Bias

Directional bias assesses *where* within the rings a person is most likely to have gone.

Factors Influencing Direction

- Last observed movement or orientation
- Witness accounts
- Known destinations or points of interest
- Psychological and behavioral profile
- Presence of transportation nodes

Application

- Assign weighted probabilities to directions (e.g., 40% north, 30% east)
- Deploy resources proportionally
- Update continuously as new data emerges

Directional bias prevents equal-effort searching of unequal probabilities.

6. LKP Operational Checklist

Step	Action	Responsible Party	Notes
1	Confirm LKP coordinates	Investigator / Family	Timestamp verification
2	Collect witness statements	Assigned interviewer	Exact times and locations
3	Secure LKP	Family / Volunteers	Prevent contamination
4	Identify terrain constraints	Search lead	Roads, water, barriers
5	Model movement radius	Analyst	Adjust for age and transport
6	Establish probability rings	Search coordinator	Define priorities
7	Apply directional bias	Lead investigator	Weight directions
8	Allocate resources	Team lead	Personnel, tools
9	Monitor and update	Operations control	Hourly reassessment
10	Document actions	LKP log officer	Full audit trail

7. Search Radius Blueprint Template

LKP-Based Search Plan (Fillable)

- LKP Coordinates:
- Time Last Seen:
- Witnesses:
- Terrain Type:
- Movement Constraints:

Estimated Radius

- Ring 1: ____ km
- Ring 2: ____ km
- Ring 3: ____ km

Directional Bias

- North: ____%
- East: ____%
- South: ____%
- West: ____%

Assigned Teams / Areas:
Resources Deployed:

- Search dogs
- Drones
- Vehicles
- Volunteers

LKP Log Notes:

8. Advanced LKP Strategies

Sequential LKP Handling

Each confirmed new sighting becomes a new LKP.

- Build separate probability rings
- Overlay models for cumulative analysis

Temporal Weighting

- Probability decays with time
- Adjust ring priorities hourly
- Integrate weather and environmental change

Communication Protocol

- Field teams report every 30–60 minutes
- All reports include GPS coordinates and timestamps

Redundant Search Avoidance

- Assign exclusive zones
- Prevent overlap unless risk escalates

Digital LKP Integration

- Phone pings
- Ride-share logs
- Social media check-ins

Digital data refines both radius and direction.

9. Family and Volunteer Guidelines

Structured volunteers amplify effectiveness; unstructured volunteers degrade it.

- Do not crowd the LKP
- Respect assigned zones
- Document all findings with time and location
- Operate in teams; safety is non-negotiable

10. Dynamic LKP Updating Plan

Time Elapsed	Action	Responsible	Notes
0–1 hr.	Confirm LKP and witnesses	Lead investigator	Initiate priority search
1–2 hr	Model radius and rings	Analyst	Deploy teams
2–4 hr	Apply directional bias	Operations lead	Reallocate resources
4–6 hr	Integrate digital data	Digital analyst	Refine zones
6–12 hr	Reassess LKP log	Control officer	Expand search
12+ hr	Process new LKPs	Lead investigator	Update plan

11. Professional Insights

- Every hour reduces probability and clarity
- Data outperforms intuition when structured correctly
- Without LKP discipline, resources scatter and leads evaporate
- Small documentation errors can misdirect entire teams

12. Key Takeaways — The LKP Method

- The LKP is the operational anchor of every search
- Probability rings turn uncertainty into structure
- Movement modeling must reflect real-world constraints
- Directional bias maximizes efficiency
- Continuous updating preserves relevance
- Checklists and logs replace panic with precision

The Last Known Point is not just a place.It is the foundation on which successful recovery is built.

5. Building the Master Case File

Turning Chaos into an Investigator-Level Dossier

Most families falter at this stage—not due to lack of care, but because they underestimate the power of structured documentation. A **Master Case File** is not a diary or scrapbook. It is a **central intelligence hub** that organizes evidence, witnesses, timelines, and digital footprints into a format that is searchable, actionable, and defensible for law enforcement or legal review.

Without a structured file:

- The Golden Hour is diluted
- Last Known Point (LKP) analysis weakens
- Leads are lost or duplicated
- Critical time is wasted

This chapter provides a professional, investigator-grade framework that families can implement immediately, even without prior investigative experience.

1. Why a Master Case File Is Critical

Missing-person investigations are inherently chaotic:

- Witnesses give conflicting accounts
- Memories degrade rapidly
- Digital evidence is overwritten
- Time-sensitive leads disappear

A Master Case File consolidates **all verified information** into one structured system, ensuring:

- Continuity across investigators, agencies, and volunteers
- Accurate, defensible timelines
- Faster operational decisions during searches
- Legal admissibility of collected information

Professional Insight: In real investigations, a well-maintained case file is often the difference between a solvable case and one that goes cold.

2. Core Sections of the Master Case File

Each Master Case File should be divided into clearly labeled sections. Incomplete sections are acceptable early on; unstructured sections are not.

A. Personal & Identification Information

Item	Required Details	Notes / Action
Full Legal Name	Legal name + aliases	Include maiden or previous names
Date of Birth	DD/MM/YYYY	Note age at disappearance
Physical Description	Height, weight, hair/ eye color	Include scars, tattoos, birthmarks
Clothing Last Worn	Full description	Include footwear, brand, condition
Recent Photographs	High-quality images	Multiple angles; day/ night
Identification Documents	Passport, ID, driver's license	Scan and preserve copies
Social Media Accounts	All platforms	Record last activity timestamps

B. Contact & Social Network Log

Name Relationship Contact Information Notes Last Contact

Guidelines:

- Begin with household members
- Expand to friends, coworkers, neighbors
- Record last interactions verbatim where possible
- Note conflicts, deviations from routine, or unusual behavior
- Always record **date and time**

C. Travel & Movement History

Date Location Transport Mode Purpose Notes

Include:

- Daily routines and commuting patterns
- Recent deviations or spontaneous trips
- Tickets, boarding passes, toll records
- Ride-share logs and vehicle GPS data

Cross-reference with LKP analysis from Chapter 4.

D. Financial Records

Record Type	Time Range	Notes	Action
Bank Statements	Last 6–12 months	Flag unusual withdrawals	Preserve copies
Credit/Debit Activity	Current	Track transactions & ATMs	Timestamp entries
Loans / Credit	Active	Note pressure or defaults	Monitor
Crypto currency	Current wallets	Capture addresses & transfers	Screenshot
Major Purchases	Recent	Electronics, travel, tickets	Attach receipts

Professional Insight: Financial behavior frequently reveals stress, intent, or movement.

E. Medical & Health Information

Category	Details	Last Update	Risk Impact	Notes
Diagnosed Conditions	Physical or mental	Date	Search priority	
Medications	Prescribed / OTC	Last refill	Time-sensitive	
Allergies	Food, drug, environmental	Current	Emergency relevance	
Physical Limitations	Mobility, vision, hearing	Current	Search radius	
Mental Health History	Depression, anxiety, therapy	Last appointment	Vulnerability	

Professional Insight: Medical data directly influences urgency, terrain choice, and survivability modeling.

F. Digital Footprint Inventory

Platform / Device	Username	Last Activity	Evidence Saved	Notes
Mobile Phone			☐	Preserve device
Laptop / Tablet			☐	Avoid tampering
Email Accounts			☐	Capture headers
Social Media			☐	Screenshot with timestamps

Preserve metadata wherever possible (timestamps, GPS, IP). Digital evidence often contradicts or clarifies witness accounts.

G. Incident & Observation Log

Date Time Observer Location Observation Action Taken

Rules:

- Chronological order only
- No speculation or emotional language
- Facts, direct quotes, and actions taken

3. Case File Organization Standards

Centralization

- One master binder or encrypted digital directory
- Clear section tabs or folders

Chronological Order

- Timelines override narratives

Version Control

- Date, time, and initials on all updates

Red-Flag Index

- Separate priority section for threats, abduction indicators, medical emergencies

Backups

- Minimum one physical and one digital copy stored separately

4. Action Plan for Families and Investigators

Step	Action	Responsible Party	Notes
1	Collect identification & photos	Family	Preserve originals
2	Compile contact lists	Family / Investigator	Verify dates
3	Gather financial records	Investigator / Family	Flag anomalies
4	Document travel & movement	Investigator	Cross-check LKP
5	Collect medical data	Family	Include providers
6	Preserve digital devices	Tech support	Do not alter
7	Build incident log	Assigned lead	Timestamp
8	Index all sections	Family	Ease retrieval
9	Maintain backups	Family	Daily
10	Update file daily	Coordinator	New leads only

5. Master Case File — Fillable Template

A. Identification

Name: ______________ DOB: ______________

Height / Weight: ______________

Hair / Eye Color: ______________

Distinguishing Marks: ______________

Last Seen Wearing: ______________

Recent Photos: ______________

B. Contacts & Social Network

(See table above)

C. Travel History

(See table above)

D. Financial Data
(See table above)
E. Medical Records
(See table above)
F. Digital Footprint
(See table above)
G. Incident Log
(See table above)
H. Priority / Red Flags

---

6. Professional Standards

- Accuracy outweighs completeness in early stages
- All documents should be dated and signed when possible
- Maintain neutrality—this is an intelligence document
- Update daily; value increases over time

7. Summary

The Master Case File underpins every subsequent investigative step:

- Enables risk profiling (Chapter 3)
- Anchors LKP and probability modeling (Chapter 4)
- Strengthens digital footprint analysis (Chapter 10)
- Supports law enforcement and media coordination
- Restores clarity and control for families

Professional Insight: Families who document early, thoroughly, and systematically are statistically far more likely to achieve recovery.

"The strongest search begins on paper—before it ever reaches the field."

6. Search Theory Professionals Use

How Experts Systematically Locate Missing Persons

Searching without a plan is chaos disguised as action. Professional search operations are not driven by urgency alone—they are grounded in **search theory**, probability, terrain analysis, and human behavior patterns.

Linear paths, grids, zones, and spirals are not arbitrary techniques. Each reflects statistical likelihood, environmental constraints, and how missing persons actually move or fail to move.

This chapter equips families, volunteers, and investigators to apply **professional search strategies** regardless of resources, terrain, or prior field experience.

1. Why Search Theory Matters

The difference between effective searching and wasted effort is **strategy**.

Search theory allows teams to:

- Maximize coverage without duplication
- Prioritize high-probability areas
- Adapt methods to terrain and environment
- Coordinate teams safely and efficiently

Without structure:

- Critical zones are missed
- Clues are trampled or lost
- Teams fatigue rapidly

- Documentation becomes unreliable

Professional Insight: Random searching reduces recovery probability. Structured searching saves time, energy, and lives.

2. Linear Search

Definition

A linear search deploys teams along a straight, defined path, moving in parallel or single-file alignment.

Use When

- Searching roads, sidewalks, or trails
- Following the Last Known Point (LKP) along a corridor
- Covering riverbanks, canals, railways, or highways

Procedure

1. Establish the path or corridor
2. Assign teams in parallel lines where possible
3. Maintain uniform spacing (typically 2–5 meters depending on visibility)
4. Advance at a steady, coordinated pace
5. Mark cleared areas on maps or logs

Advantages

- Simple to organize
- Highly effective in predictable corridors
- Easy to document and brief

Limitations

- Inefficient for large open or irregular terrain
- Reduced effectiveness in dense vegetation or cluttered environments

3. Grid Search

Definition

A grid search divides the search area into uniform squares or rectangles, ensuring systematic, complete coverage.

Use When

- Searching open fields, parks, or urban blocks
- Terrain allows consistent visibility
- Thorough coverage is required

Procedure

1. Map and divide the area into grid units
2. Assign teams to each grid square
3. Sweep each square methodically from one boundary to the other
4. Log completion before moving on

Advantages

- High probability of full-area coverage
- Easy to assign volunteers and track progress
- Works well with mixed-skill teams

Limitations

- Resource-intensive
- Requires maps, coordination, and discipline

4. Zone Search

Definition

A zone search segments a large or complex area into sectors, each managed by a designated leader.

Use When

- Covering large or varied terrain
- Deploying multiple teams
- Risk and probability vary by area

Procedure

1. Divide the area into logical zones
2. Assign teams and a leader to each zone
3. Establish central command communication
4. Reallocate teams dynamically based on findings

Advantages

- Scalable and adaptable
- Prioritizes high-probability sectors
- Improves accountability and reporting

Limitations

- Requires accurate mapping

- Dependent on leadership and communication discipline

5. Spiral Method

Definition

The spiral method expands outward (or inward) from a known point in concentric paths.

Use When

- LKP is confirmed and precise
- Search area is small to medium
- Individual may be stationary, injured, or disoriented

Procedure

1. Begin at the LKP
2. Expand search radius in controlled increments
3. Maintain consistent spacing between searchers
4. Move slowly to detect subtle indicators

Advantages

- Concentrates effort where probability is highest
- Highly effective in early search phases
- Minimizes wasted coverage

Limitations

- Inefficient for large areas
- Requires a reliable starting point

6. Terrain-Adaptive Search Strategies

No single method fits all environments. Professional searches adapt strategy to terrain.

Terrain Type	Recommended Strategy	Notes
Urban Streets	Linear + Zone	Account for buildings, alleys, traffic
Parks / Fields	Grid + Zone	Adjust spacing for vegetation
Forested Areas	Spiral + Zone	Spacing 2–3m; scent dogs recommended
Mountains	Zone + Contour Sweep	Assign teams by slope and elevation
Water Bodies	Linear Shore Search	Deploy boats, sonar, drones
Mixed Terrain	Hybrid Approach	Prioritize probability zones

Professional Tip: Adjust team spacing continuously. Dense terrain demands tighter spacing; open terrain allows wider coverage.

7. Team Coordination and Safety

Effective searches prioritize coordination and responder safety:

- Assign a leader to every team or zone
- Maintain continuous radio or mobile communication
- Log every cleared area
- Rotate teams to prevent fatigue and tunnel vision
- Ensure water, first aid, and navigation tools are available
- Document clues immediately and preserve context

Remember: Efficiency comes from structure—not speed.

8. Field Search Checklist

Task	Responsible Party	Notes
Confirm LKP	Lead Investigator	Record coordinates & time
Select Search Method	Lead Investigator	Linear, grid, zone, spiral, hybrid
Assign Teams	Operations Lead	Include volunteers and specialists
Set Team Spacing	Team Leaders	Terrain and visibility dependent
Equip Searchers	All Members	Radios, maps, GPS, first aid
Record Coverage	Documentation Officer	Mark cleared areas
Log Observations	Team Leaders	Tracks, items, witnesses
Rotate Teams	Operations Lead	Prevent fatigue
Debrief	All Teams	Update Master Case File
Adjust Plan	Operations Lead	Integrate new intelligence

9. Search Deployment Plan Template

Search Operation — Missing Person

- LKP Coordinates: ______________________________
- Terrain Type: ______________________________
- Search Method: ☐ Linear ☐ Grid ☐ Zone ☐ Spiral ☐ Hybrid
- Number of Teams: ______________________________
- Team Leaders: ______________________________
- Team Spacing: ______________________________
- Resources Deployed: ☐ Search Dogs ☐ Drones ☐ Vehicles ☐ Volunteers

- Probability Zones:
    - Ring 1 (High): ___ km
    - Ring 2 (Medium): ___ km
    - Ring 3 (Low): ___ km
- Reporting Interval: Every ___ minutes
- Documentation Officer: ______________________________

10. Professional Insights

- **High-probability zones first:** Begin near the LKP and along expected routes
- **Systematic coverage:** Missed or overlapping areas reduce success rates
- **Documentation:** Logs become critical during law enforcement transfer
- **Flexibility:** Adjust methods as terrain, weather, or intelligence changes

Pro Tip: Volunteers are most effective when given structure. Chaos lowers recovery probability.

11. Summary

Professional search theory is the backbone of effective field operations. Key takeaways:

- Select search methods based on probability, terrain, and resources
- Apply linear, grid, zone, spiral, or hybrid strategies appropriately
- Adapt continuously to environmental and intelligence changes

- Maintain leadership, communication, and documentation

"A search without theory is hope in motion. A search with strategy is action with results."

When a person goes missing, public perception often imagines immediate, dramatic police action—sirens, helicopters, instant digital surveillance. In reality, missing-person investigations follow **structured, procedural workflows** governed by risk assessment, legal thresholds, and resource availability.

Understanding how police actually operate is critical. Families who grasp this process provide **better intelligence**, coordinate more effectively, and avoid actions that unintentionally slow escalation.

This chapter demystifies police procedures and shows how to work *with* the system rather than against it.

1. Breaking the Myths

Myth: Police immediately launch full-scale searches for every missing person.

Reality: Cases are triaged based on age, vulnerability, risk indicators, and circumstances.

Myth: Reporting a missing adult is automatically delayed or dismissed.

Reality: Adult cases escalate rapidly when danger, coercion, or health risks are evident.

Myth: Families can pressure police into faster action.

Reality: Law enforcement response is governed by documentation, risk thresholds, and protocol—not perceived urgency.

Key Insight: Families who provide structured, actionable intelligence accelerate response *within* the system.

2. Intake Procedure

The intake process forms the foundation of the entire investigation. Errors or omissions here can delay escalation.

Step-by-Step Intake Workflow

1. Initial Contact

- File a report at a police station or authorized digital portal
- Provide identifying information: name, age, physical description, recent photo

2. Verification of Circumstances

- Determine whether the individual is missing, delayed, or voluntarily absent
- Review prior disappearances, routines, and behavioral history
- Assess medical or mental health factors

3. Documentation

- Information entered into official databases (local, regional, national)
- Incident or case number generated for tracking

4. Initial Risk Assessment

- Case graded based on age, health, environment, and threat indicators
- High-risk cases flagged for immediate escalation

5. Assignment of Investigation Team

- Case assigned to an officer or detective

- Specialized units engaged as required (K9, cyber, forensic)

3. Priority Grading

Police determine response speed and resource allocation through priority grading.

Priority Level	Typical Characteristics	Response Actions
Critical / Top Priority	Child under 12, elderly, medical risk, suicidal ideation, evidence of abduction	Immediate search, multi-agency alerts, K9/drones, media activation
High Priority	Teen, vulnerable adult, mental health concerns, suspicious circumstances	Rapid investigation, initial search, digital analysis
Medium Priority	Adult, unclear voluntary absence, minor risk factors	Documentation, monitoring, routine follow-up
Low Priority	Adult voluntary absence, prior history of leaving	Case logged, periodic review, minimal resources

Professional Insight: Priority is dynamic. New evidence—financial anomalies, digital activity, confirmed sightings—can rapidly escalate a case.

4. Resource Allocation

Resources are deployed according to priority, geography, and availability.

Resource Categories

- **Field Teams:** Patrol officers, detectives, K9, search specialists
- **Technical Units:** CCTV review, phone analysis, digital

forensics

- **Coordination:** Dispatch, operations command, volunteer management
- **Support Units:** Medical, forensic, psychological and family liaison

Typical Allocation Model

Case Priority	Field Teams	Digital Forensics	Coordination	Additional Support
Critical	5+ teams, continuous shifts	Immediate	Central command, daily briefings	K9, drones, media
High	2–3 teams, rotating shifts	Rapid	Ops support	Limited K9, volunteers
Medium	1–2 teams	Standard	Ops support	Volunteer coordination
Low	Single officer	Routine	Minimal	Family liaison

5. Why Some Cases Escalate Faster

Cases move quickly when **actionable risk indicators** are present:

- **Immediate Threats:** Violence, abduction, coercion
- **Vulnerability:** Children, elderly, disabled, suicidal individuals
- **Digital Evidence:** Phone pings, financial transactions, social media activity
- **Verified Sightings:** CCTV, transit records, witness confirmation
- **Environmental Risk:** Dangerous terrain, extreme weather,

urban hazards

- **Public Alerts:** Amber Alerts, media appeals, public tips

Key Insight: Escalation is evidence-driven—not emotion-driven.

6. Insider Workflow (Operational View)

```
[Report Filed / Initial Contact]
    |
    v
    [Verification & Intake]
    |
    v
    [Initial Risk Assessment]—-> [Assign Priority Grade]
    | |
    v v
    [Assign Investigation Team] [Allocate Resources]
    | |
    v v
    [Field Investigation Begins] <-> [Digital / CCTV Analysis]
    |
    v
    [Ops Command Updates]
    |
    v
    [Adjust Priority / Redeploy]
    |
    v
    [Escalation / Media Alerts]
    |
    v
    [Continuous Documentation]
```

How Families Use This:

- Know *who* to give information to
- Understand *when* updates matter
- Realize how missing details slow escalation

7. Family & Investigator Actions during Police Operations

- Provide a structured **Master Case File** (Chapter 5)
- Flag red-risk indicators immediately
- Share LKP and probability analysis (Chapter 4)
- Coordinate volunteer efforts through police command
- Document all police communications and updates

Reminder: Families are operational partners—not adversaries.

8. Police Coordination Tips for Families

- Report **facts only**, not assumptions
- Obtain the incident number and lead officer's name
- Keep copies of all submitted documents
- Clarify update frequency expectations
- Share new evidence immediately
- Avoid contaminating potential evidence sites

9. Summary

Police investigations are structured, prioritized, and resource-dependent.

Key principles:

- Intake accuracy determines investigation trajectory
- Priority grading drives speed and scale
- Resource allocation follows risk, not pressure

- Families who understand workflow improve outcomes

"Knowledge of procedure is power. The better you understand how investigators think, the stronger your partnership becomes."

Key Takeaways

- Do not assume immediate action—focus on structured intelligence
- Use the Master Case File and LKP analysis to drive escalation
- Understand what elevates priority
- Coordinate calmly, document everything, and work as a partner

7. Working with Law Enforcement (Not Against Them)

Effective Collaboration to Maximize Recovery Potential

Missing-person cases succeed through **partnership**, not confrontation. Families and volunteers often act from urgency or fear, which—without structure—can unintentionally slow investigations or fracture trust.

This chapter provides **clear communication protocols, escalation logic, legal awareness, and official templates** so your involvement accelerates police action rather than impedes it.

1. Communication Protocol

Objective: Ensure information flow is timely, accurate, and actionable.

Best Practices

Designate a Single Point of Contact (SPOC)

- Assign one family member or lead volunteer to communicate with police
- Prevents duplicated, conflicting, or fragmented information

Use Formal Channels

- Submit information in writing or via authorized digital portals
- Document every interaction (date, time, officer, summary)

Structure Information Submission

- Always include: LKP analysis, Master Case File excerpts, sightings, and digital evidence
- Submit verifiable facts only—no speculation

Set Update Expectations

- Confirm communication frequency (hourly, daily, milestone-based)
- Understand that tactical details may not be shareable

Know Escalation Protocols

- Escalation is procedural, not adversarial (see Section 2)

2. Escalation Triggers

Escalation is a **formal request** for additional resources or authority when risk increases or progress stalls.

Trigger	**Recommended Action**
Child under 12 missing	Immediate escalation to high-priority or child protection unit
Elderly or medical risk	Request medical / welfare priority flag
Evidence of abduction, threats, violence	Escalate to criminal investigation / rapid response
Delays or non-response	Request supervisory review
Cross-jurisdictional indicators	Notify regional or national agencies
Digital or financial anomalies	Engage cybercrime / financial units

Professional Tip: Escalation aligned with protocol is cooperation—not confrontation.

3. Legal Rights of Families

Understanding your rights strengthens collaboration and protects the investigation.

- **Right to File a Report:** No agency may refuse a missing-person report
- **Right to Updates:** Families are entitled to reasonable status updates and officer contact details
- **Right to Submit Evidence:** Physical and digital evidence can be formally logged
- **Right to Legal Representation:** Especially relevant for minors or high-risk cases
- **Right to Escalate:** Formal appeal to supervisors or higher authorities is lawful
- **Right to Transparency:** Decisions regarding prioritization must be documented

Professional Insight: Respectful assertion of rights increases clarity and trust.

4. When to Engage Higher Agencies

Local police may lack jurisdiction or specialized resources. Escalate when appropriate.

Scenario	Recommended Agency
Cross-city or interstate disappearance	Regional / state task force
International travel suspected	Interpol or federal agency
Cyber or financial evidence	Cybercrime / fraud units
Kidnapping or organized crime	Specialized investigative units
Amber Alert activation	National child protection authorities

Tip: Provide a complete Master Case File and LKP analysis to accelerate action.

5. Official Interaction Template (Fillable)

Official Communication Form — Missing Person Case

Field	Details
Date & Time	______________________
Officer / Department	______________________
Incident Number	______________________
SPOC Name	______________________
Missing Person	______________________
LKP Coordinates	______________________
Evidence Submitted	______________________
Observations / Tips	______________________
Requests / Actions	☐ Escalation ☐ Resources ☐ Update ☐ Other _____
Follow-Up Date	______________________
Notes	______________________

Usage Guidelines

- Complete after every information exchange
- Retain a copy in the Master Case File
- Reference the incident number in all correspondence

6. Collaboration Best Practices

- Respect the chain of command
- Provide structured, actionable intelligence
- Document every interaction
- Integrate volunteers only through official coordination
- Maintain transparency and honesty
- Escalate promptly when verified risk increases

7. Insider Professional Insights

- Organized families receive faster, clearer responses
- Uncoordinated searches often disrupt evidence and operations
- Structured communication increases attention and effectiveness
- Escalation is a strategic tool—not a complaint mechanism

8. Quick Checklist — Working WITH Law Enforcement

Task	Responsible	Notes
Designate SPOC	Family / Lead Volunteer	Single communicator
Prepare Master Case File	Family / Investigator	Include LKP
Submit Information Formally	SPOC	Time stamped
Verify Police Contact	SPOC	Officer & department
Track Follow-Ups	SPOC	Log updates
Identify Escalation Triggers	SPOC	Risk indicators
Engage Higher Agency	SPOC	Full documentation
Maintain Professional Tone	SPOC	Factual, calm
Integrate Volunteers	Liaison	Official tasks only
Update Master Case File	Family	Daily or as needed

9. Summary

Effective collaboration with law enforcement is as critical as field search operations.

Key points:

- Families are partners—structured communication accelerates response
- Use SPOC, formal submissions, and documented follow-ups
- Know escalation triggers and legal rights
- Escalate respectfully with verified evidence
- Maintain accurate logs and daily case updates

Professional Insight: Structured cooperation is the difference between a stalled case and a coordinated recovery.

8. Intelligence Gathering From Social Circles

Unlocking the Hidden Clues Friends and Acquaintances Hold

Friends, neighbors, colleagues, and even casual acquaintances often know more than they initially disclose. In missing-person cases, breakthroughs frequently come from **subtle details**—changes in routine, quiet conflicts, new relationships, or mounting stressors.

This chapter provides **structured, professional methods** to gather social-circle intelligence while preserving trust, accuracy, and evidentiary value.

1. Principles of Social-Circle Intelligence

- **Memory is reconstructive:** Recollection improves with structure and context.
- **Information may be minimized:** Loyalty, fear, embarrassment, or self-protection can limit disclosure.
- **Consistency increases reliability:** Multiple independent sources strengthen confidence.
- **Non-confrontation works:** Aggression reduces cooperation and distorts recall.
- **Documentation is mandatory:** Record every statement with date, time, and source.

Professional Insight: Intelligence is not gossip. It is verifiable, structured information that guides risk assessment and search decisions.

2. Cognitive Interviewing

Definition: A structured recall technique used by law enforcement and intelligence professionals to enhance memory without introducing bias.

Step-by-Step Method

1. Build Rapport

- Begin with neutral conversation
- Reduce anxiety; establish psychological safety

2. Context Reinstatement

- Ask the interviewee to mentally recreate the setting of last contact
- Prompt sensory details: sights, sounds, weather, emotions

3. Report Everything

- Encourage inclusion of all details, even seemingly trivial ones
- Reinforce that small details may matter

4. Reverse-Order Recall

- Ask the person to recount events backward
- This often triggers forgotten details

5. Change Perspective

- Ask what others present might have noticed
- Reveals overlooked observations

6. Avoid Leading Questions

- Use open-ended, neutral phrasing
- Prevents contamination of memory

3. Statement Comparison

Objective: Identify corroboration, contradictions, and gaps across sources.

Process

1. Collect statements from friends, coworkers, neighbors, acquaintances
2. Align statements chronologically
3. Categorize findings:
    - **Agreements:** Corroborated information
    - **Contradictions:** Require clarification
    - **Omissions:** Potentially forgotten or withheld details
4. Cross-reference with:
    - Master Case File (Chapter 5)
    - LKP analysis (Chapter 4)
    - Digital records and timestamps

Tip: Minor inconsistencies are normal. Focus on deviations that affect **time, location, or risk.**

4. Detecting Deception and Omission

Most misleading information stems from fear or loyalty—not malice. Handle carefully.

Warning Indicators

- Persistent vagueness or repeated "I don't remember"
- Changing details across retellings
- Overemphasis on irrelevant information
- Avoidance of dates, times, or locations

Professional Response

- Remain neutral and patient
- Rephrase questions instead of repeating them
- Seek corroboration through evidence or other witnesses
- Never accuse—frame inquiries as fact-finding

5. Structured Interview Question Bank

Designed for families, volunteers, and investigators. Use verbatim when possible.

A. General Questions

Question	Purpose	Notes
When was the last time you saw or spoke with them?	Establish LKP	Exact time & location
Did anything seem unusual in their behavior?	Detect stressors	Specific incidents
Did they mention plans, trips, or meetings?	Identify movement	Verify calendars/tickets
Were there conflicts or tensions?	Behavioral context	Names involved
Did they mention anyone new in their life?	External influence	Social, romantic, work

B. Movement & Routine

Question	Purpose	Notes
Which places did they visit recently?	Pattern recognition	Compare to probability rings
Any new or unusual habits?	Voluntary indicators	Cross-check others
Did they miss expected appointments?	Deviation detection	Verify records
Any travel plans or bookings?	Expanded LKP	Request proof
Did they use a vehicle or public transport?	Movement reconstruction	GPS / ride-share

C. Social & Digital Context

Question	Purpose	Notes
Any changes in social media use?	Digital anomalies	Capture screenshots
Unusual messages or calls?	Threat detection	Preserve evidence
Financial worries discussed?	Stress indicators	Corroborate records
New acquaintances or strangers?	Risk actors	Map relationships
Expressed fears or conflicts?	Behavioral signals	Dates & names

D. Observational & Environmental

Question	Purpose	Notes
Items missing or moved?	Pre-event clues	Dates
Personal belongings left behind?	Voluntary risk	Photograph
Unusual visitors or deliveries?	Third-party involvement	Follow-up
Signs of distress or injury?	Risk scoring	Medical relevance
Talk of disappearing or leaving?	Intent signals	Corroborate

6. Documentation Template

Interview Record — Social Circle Intelligence

Field	Entry
Date	______________________
Time	______________________
Interviewee	______________________
Relationship	______________________
Last Seen Interaction	______________________
Key Observations	______________________
Evidence Submitted	______________________

Instructions

- Complete immediately after the interview
- Capture verbatim quotes when possible
- Timestamp all evidence (messages, photos, emails)
- Link each record to the Master Case File

7. Field Implementation Tips

- Assign a consistent interviewer for continuity
- Conduct interviews in neutral, private settings
- Build rapport before questioning
- Avoid interrogative tone; encourage narrative recall
- Integrate findings with LKP mapping, timelines, and risk scoring

8. Summary

Social circles are critical intelligence sources when approached systematically.

Key points:

- Use cognitive interviewing to improve recall
- Compare statements to identify corroboration and gaps
- Detect deception through pattern recognition—not accusation
- Document and corroborate every statement
- Integrate findings into search planning and risk analysis

Professional Insight: The clues that solve cases are often buried in casual conversations. Structure, documentation, and corroboration turn fragments into intelligence.

9. The Digital Footprint Hunt

How Modern Investigations Begin Online

In modern missing-person investigations, digital evidence is often the **first, fastest, and most actionable source of intelligence**. Phones, computers, cloud services, social platforms, transportation apps, and financial systems can reveal movement, intent, stressors, contacts, and third-party involvement.

This chapter presents a **professional, preservation-first methodology** for identifying, securing, extracting, documenting, and handing over digital evidence **without contaminating data or creating legal exposure**.

1. Understanding the Digital Landscape

Scope of Digital Footprints

Category	Examples	Investigative Value
Phone activity	Calls, SMS, app usage, GPS	Movement, contacts, timing
Social media	Posts, DMs, metadata, logins	Intent, relationships, threats
Cloud data	Photos, notes, calendars, backups	Historical context, locations
Transport logs	Ride-share, tickets, tolls	Route reconstruction
Financial activity	Cards, wallets, online payments	Stressors, travel, coercion

Professional Insight: Digital evidence is perishable. Logs overwrite, accounts change, and cloud data syncs automatically. **Preservation must occur immediately.**

2. Device & Account Preservation (CRITICAL FIRST STEP)

Device Preservation Checklist

Task	Required Action	Responsible Party	Status	Notes
Secure mobile devices	Enable Airplane Mode; disable Wi-Fi/ Bluetooth	Family / Tech Lead	☐	Do not reboot
Secure computers/ tablets	Disconnect from all networks	Family / Tech Lead	☐	Preserve state
Prevent unauthorized access	Store in sealed location	SPOC	☐	Limit handlers
Document identifiers	Model, serial, IMEI, OS	Tech Lead	☐	Photograph labels
Preserve SIM cards	Remove only if advised	Tech Lead	☐	Bag & label
Chain of custody	Log every handling event	SPOC	☐	Mandatory

Warning: Power cycling or unlocking devices can permanently erase logs.

3. Credentials, Consent & Legal Access

Access Control Checklist

Task	Action Required	Responsible Party	Status	Notes
Collect credentials	Usernames, passwords	Family / Legal	☐	Store securely
Identify 2FA methods	SMS, authenticator, device	Tech Lead	☐	Prevent lockout
Verify account ownership	Name, recovery email/phone	SPOC	☐	Needed for providers
Confirm legal authority	Family consent / legal review	Legal	☐	Avoid violations

4. Phone Pings & Location Intelligence

Location Intelligence Checklist

Task	Action Required	Responsible Party	Status	Notes
Carrier request	Last tower pings & times	Police / Investigator	☐	Legal request
Device GPS logs	Google Timeline / Apple Find My	Tech Lead	☐	Export raw
Map movements	Overlay on routes/ terrain	Investigator	☐	Visual map
Cross-reference travel	Ride-share, tickets, tolls	Investigator	☐	Identify gaps

Professional Tip: Even powered-off devices may retain cached location data in apps or cloud backups.

5. Social Media & Communications Analysis

Social Intelligence Checklist

Task	Action Required	Responsible Party	Status	Notes
Account inventory	Social, messaging, gaming	SPOC	☐	Include inactive
Capture last activity	Posts, stories, DMs	Tech Lead	☐	Screenshot + export
Identify new contacts	Unknown/recent profiles	Investigator	☐	Flag interviews
Preserve deleted items	Archives, trash, hidden chats	Tech Lead	☐	Time-sensitive
Export conversations	PDF/CSV with timestamps	Tech Lead	☐	Do not edit

6. Metadata & Digital Artifacts

Metadata Handling Checklist

Task	Action Required	Responsible Party	Status	Notes
Preserve originals	Photos, videos, docs	Tech Lead	☐	No edits
Extract metadata	EXIF, timestamps, device IDs	Tech Lead	☐	Forensic tools
Identify capture locations	GPS from files	Investigator	☐	Validate sightings
Validate timelines	Compare with statements	Investigator	☐	Note conflicts

7. Cloud Backups & Remote Data

Cloud Extraction Checklist

Task	Action Required	Responsible Party	Status	Notes
Access cloud accounts	iCloud, Google, One Drive	Tech Lead	☐	Authorized only
Download backups	Photos, notes, calendars	Tech Lead	☐	Keep structure
Extract app backups	Messaging archives	Tech Lead	☐	Often missed
Verify integrity	File size / hash	Tech Lead	☐	Police handover

Professional Insight: Cloud data often contains evidence missing from the physical device.

8. Transportation & Financial Records

Movement & Transaction Checklist

Task	Action Required	Responsible Party	Status	Notes
Review bank activity	Cards, wallets, UPI	Investigator / Family	☐	Flag anomalies
Collect ride-share logs	Uber, Lyft, Ola, Grab	Investigator	☐	GPS routes
Review tickets	Bus, rail, flights	Investigator	☐	Missed travel
Check rentals & fuel	Car hire, tolls	Investigator	☐	Movement clues

9. Documentation & Case Integration

Documentation Checklist

Task	Action Required	Responsible Party	Status	Notes
Centralize evidence	Secure repository	SPOC	☐	Structured folders
Timestamp everything	Date, time, source	SPOC	☐	Mandatory
Update Master Case File	Link digital findings	SPOC	☐	Chapter 5
Police handover	Assigned officer only	SPOC	☐	Avoid duplication
Maintain daily log	Actions & findings	SPOC	☐	Supports escalation

10. Professional Implementation Guidance

- Preserve first; analyze second.
- Never edit originals or rely solely on screenshots.
- Coordinate provider requests with law enforcement.
- Digital findings frequently **change risk grading, search radius, and escalation priority**.

11. Summary

Digital footprints are foundational to modern missing-person investigations.

Key Takeaways:

- Treat digital evidence as fragile and time-sensitive.
- Follow a structured workflow: **preservation → extraction → documentation → handover**.
- Integrate digital findings with LKP analysis, social intelligence, and field search planning.

Professional Insight: In modern cases, the search often begins online. Correct preservation shapes the entire investigation.

10. Why People Vanish

Understanding the Human Mind behind Disappearance

Not all missing-person cases are criminal events. A significant percentage result from psychological strain, social pressure, or financial instability. Understanding *why* an individual disappears is critical for predicting movement, assessing risk, and allocating investigative and search resources effectively.

This chapter examines the primary behavioral drivers behind voluntary disappearance and provides structured predictor frameworks and operational checklists for investigative and field use.

1. Escape Psychology

Voluntary disappearance frequently occurs when personal stressors exceed an individual's coping capacity. The decision to leave is often deliberate, partially concealed, and psychologically motivated.

Common Triggers

- Emotional overload (depression, anxiety, unresolved conflict)
- Perceived threats or fear of harm
- Desire to escape responsibility, legal exposure, or social identity

Behavioral Indicators

Behavior	Description	Predictive Value
Sudden withdrawal	Abrupt reduction in communication with close contacts	High
Emotional volatility	Irritability, despair, or emotional outbursts	Medium
Selective packing	Taking essential or symbolic personal items only	High
Digital disengagement	Social media or messaging activity stops	High
Verbal hints	Statements about needing a "fresh start"	Medium

Professional Insight: Voluntary escapes are rarely impulsive. Most involve partial planning and subtle behavioral signals prior to departure.

2. Financial Collapse

Economic stress is a major driver of adult disappearances, particularly when exposure or loss of status is imminent.

Contributing Factors

- Severe debt or bankruptcy
- Fraud or embezzlement exposure
- Job loss or inability to meet financial obligations

Financial Behavioral Signs

Sign	Observation	Investigative Action
Asset liquidation	Sale of valuables or rapid cash withdrawals	Trace financial transactions
Account closures	Bank, subscription, or payment account shutdowns	Document timing and sequence
Lifestyle disruption	Abandoned property or abrupt relocation	Review LKP and travel history
Hidden transactions	Crypto currency or offshore activity	Conduct forensic financial analysis

Professional Insight: Financially driven disappearances often aim at concealment or temporary withdrawal rather than self-harm.

3. Secret Relationships

Undisclosed relationships—romantic, social, or criminal—can precipitate sudden disappearance and increase risk exposure.

Observed Patterns

Relationship Type	Behavioral Indicators	Investigative Notes
New romantic involvement	Late-night calls, unexplained absences	Review messages, ride-share, social media
Abusive or coercive partner	Fear responses, avoidance behaviors	Prioritize safety and risk assessment
Secret social groups	Routine disruption, withdrawal	Interview associates and peers
Criminal association	Unexplained cash flow or travel	Cross-check law enforcement databases

Professional Insight: These cases may appear voluntary but frequently involve coercion, danger, or exploitation.

4. Identity Reinvention

Some individuals intentionally disappear to construct a new identity, abandoning social, professional, and digital ties.

Identity Reinvention Indicators

- Closure of longstanding accounts
- Creation of new or anonymous digital personas
- Abandonment of residence, vehicle, or employment
- Travel to off-grid or low-trace locations

Behavioral Predictor Chart — Identity Reinvention

Behavioral Marker	Likelihood of Vanishing	Notes
Closure of legacy accounts	High	Intentional footprint suppression
Minimal trace communication	High	Indicates pre-departure planning
Burner phones or emails	Medium	Operational preparation
Property disposal or packing	Medium	Often disguised as routine
Social media inactivity	High	Common planning-stage marker

Professional Insight: Identity reinvention leaves a calculated but detectable trail through social and digital analysis.

5. Behavioral Predictor Framework

This framework supports structured risk assessment and prioritization.

Category	Low Risk	Medium Risk	High Risk
Voluntary Escape	Occasional withdrawal	Reduced contact, minor packing	Explicit intent, total digital blackout
Financial Collapse	Minor debt	Asset liquidation	Hidden accounts, bankruptcy
Relationship Pressure	Social tension	Repeated conflicts	Abusive or secretive relationships
Identity Reinvention	Expressed dissatisfaction	Routine disruption	Account deletion, new identities
Emotional/ Psychological	Mood changes	Isolation, irritability	Severe depression, suicidal ideation

Usage Guidance: Plot indicators to assign behavioral probability zones and refine investigative focus.

6. Integration with Investigation

Behavioral analysis must be combined with:

- Last Known Point (LKP)
- Social circle intelligence
- Digital footprint analysis

Search Strategy Alignment

Dominant Driver	Primary Focus
Voluntary escape	Friend networks, public transport, off-grid zones
Financial collapse	Banking activity, transaction logs, travel records
Identity reinvention	Online presence, digital artifacts, alias activity

Update the Master Case File with behavioral findings for coordinated law enforcement or PI collaboration.

7. Field Action Checklist — Behavioral Analysis

Task	Responsible Party	Notes
Collect behavioral history	Family / Investigator	Statements, journals, social media
Map behavioral risk categories	Investigator	Escape, financial, relational, identity
Identify key triggers	Investigator / Police	Stressors, debt, conflicts
Update Master Case File	SPOC	Include charts and evidence
Correlate with LKP and digital data	Investigator	Refine search zones
Adjust search strategy	Operations Lead	Match terrain and likelihood

8. Professional Insight

- Behavioral analysis significantly increases recovery probability
- Ignoring psychological drivers leads to misallocated resources
- Integrated behavioral, social, and digital intelligence enables 360-degree investigation
- Predictor frameworks assist law enforcement in urgency and risk prioritization

9. Summary

Disappearances result from intersecting psychological, social, and financial pressures. Escape psychology, financial collapse, secret relationships, and identity reinvention each provide measurable predictive markers.

Structured behavioral frameworks allow investigators and families to assess risk, refine LKP analysis, and deploy targeted search strategies.

Professional Insight: Every disappearance leaves a psychological footprint. Decoding it is as critical as tracing physical or digital evidence.

11. Suicide vs. Staged Disappearance Indicators

Critical Distinctions for Life-Saving Intervention

Not all disappearances are voluntary or benign. Some involve imminent risk of self-harm, while others are deliberately staged to mislead family, friends, or authorities. Differentiating between these possibilities is time-sensitive and operationally critical. Early, structured assessment can mean the difference between recovery and fatality.

This chapter provides a disciplined framework to distinguish suicide risk from staged disappearance, integrating behavioral, social, and digital intelligence to guide urgent decision-making.

1. Core Principles

- **Immediate assessment is critical:** The first hours after disappearance may determine life or death.
- **Behavioral indicators are often subtle:** Look beyond surface-level explanations.
- **Integrated intelligence is essential:** Correlate findings with Social Circle Intelligence (Chapter 9), Digital Footprint Analysis (Chapter 10), and Behavioral Predictors (Chapter 11).
- **Documentation is mandatory:** Every observation must be recorded for investigators and mental health professionals.

Professional Insight: Early identification of high-risk individuals enables rapid intervention and prioritization of field resources.

2. Suicide Risk Indicators

Suicidal disappearances often present with converging behavioral, emotional, and environmental signals.

Key Warning Signs

Category	Indicators	Notes
Verbal	Expressions of hopelessness, statements such as "I wish I weren't here," final goodbyes	Record wording verbatim
Behavioral	Social withdrawal, neglect of hygiene, giving away possessions	Frequently precedes disappearance
Emotional	Depression, anxiety, irritability, emotional flatness	Track recent changes
Digital	Farewell messages, posts implying closure or endings	Preserve screenshots and metadata
Environmental	Access to lethal means or high-risk locations	Identify and notify authorities
History	Prior suicide attempts or self-harm	Critical for risk scoring

Professional Tip: The presence of multiple indicators significantly increases urgency. Treat such cases as critical until ruled out.

3. Staged Disappearance Indicators

A staged disappearance is intentionally designed to misdirect observers regarding intent or outcome. These cases are often voluntary and planned, though they may still involve secondary risks.

Common Indicators

Category	Indicators	Notes
Preparation	Systematic removal of belongings, planned routes	Partial trails may be intentional
Communication	Contradictory or misleading messages	Verify timestamps and origins
Digital Activity	Sudden account deactivation or anomalous logins	Suggests concealment planning
Financial	Limited withdrawals, prepaid services	Indicates control rather than panic
Social	Selective goodbyes, muted emotional signals	Often sensed by close contacts

Professional Insight: Staged disappearances rarely involve immediate suicidal intent but can delay emergency response if misinterpreted.

4. Rapid Suicide vs. Staged Disappearance Risk Assessment Model

This scoring model supports rapid triage and urgency determination.

Factor	Observation Range	Score (0–3)	Notes
Verbal suicidal statements	None → explicit	0–3	Document exact phrasing
Behavioral withdrawal	Minimal → extreme	0–3	Include hygiene and isolation
Digital footprint	Active → farewell content	0–3	Preserve logs and screenshots
Access to means	None → imminent	0–3	Medications, weapons, locations
Financial patterns	Normal → prepaid travel	0–3	Helps differentiate staging
Social interaction	Normal → selective goodbyes	0–3	Cross-check witnesses
Planning evidence	None → extensive	0–3	Travel, luggage, alt accounts

Score Interpretation

- **0–5:** Low risk — likely voluntary; continue monitoring
- **6–12:** Medium risk — escalate investigation and maintain contact
- **13–21:** High risk — treat as life-threatening emergency; deploy immediate response

5. Early Action Steps

- **Immediate notification:** Alert law enforcement, medical, or mental health professionals when high risk is identified.
- **Preserve evidence:** Maintain all digital and physical materials intact.

- **Contact social circle:** Confirm recent statements, mood, and interactions.
- **Document continuously:** Each observation contributes to cumulative risk assessment.
- **Coordinate search operations:** Deploy teams based on LKP, behavioral indicators, and digital data.

6. Integration with Other Chapters

Intelligence Source	Contribution
Behavioral Analysis (Ch. 11)	Identifies stressors, escape patterns
Social Intelligence (Ch. 9)	Validates statements, detects deception
Digital Footprint (Ch. 10)	Reveals messages, activity, travel
Master Case File (Ch. 5)	Centralizes risk scores and evidence

Professional Insight: No single indicator is decisive. Predictive accuracy emerges from cross-domain pattern recognition.

7. Field Risk Checklist

Task	Responsible Party	Notes
Complete suicide/staged risk score	Investigator / SPOC	Use structured model
Preserve digital communications	Family / Technical support	Capture timestamps
Collect personal effects	Family / Police	Journals, purchases, notes
Verify LKP and routes	Investigator / Field team	Correlate with social data
Notify authorities	SPOC / Police liaison	Immediate if high risk
Monitor social circle	Family / Investigator	Track contradictions
Update Master Case File	SPOC	Log all new findings

8. Professional Insight

- Time sensitivity is paramount; early recognition saves lives
- Assumption-based action increases risk and misallocates resources
- Structured differentiation guides law enforcement urgency and deployment

9. Summary

Distinguishing suicide risk from staged disappearance is essential for effective, life-saving intervention. Structured risk scoring enables families and investigators to prioritize action objectively.

Integrated behavioral, social, and digital intelligence provides a 360-degree situational understanding. Accurate documentation, rapid communication with authorities, and adherence to protocol transform urgency into effective response.

Professional Insight: Every hour matters. A disciplined, evidence-based approach turns uncertainty into decisive, potentially life-saving action.

12. Criminal Abduction Patterns

Understanding Offender Logic to Interrupt the Crime

Criminal abductions are statistically rare compared to voluntary disappearances, yet they represent the highest-risk category due to the rapid escalation of harm. When abduction occurs, speed, pattern recognition, and structured response are decisive. Contrary to public perception, most abductions are not random acts—they follow identifiable behavioral, geographic, and situational patterns.

This chapter equips families, investigators, journalists, and law enforcement with practical frameworks to recognize abduction indicators early and shift a case from uncertainty to focused, high-probability action.

Core Principle: Offenders may be emotionally inconsistent, but they are operationally predictable.

1. Offender Logic — How Abductions Actually Occur

Abductions emerge where opportunity, victim vulnerability, and offender confidence intersect. Understanding offender motivation is essential for predicting victim movement and escalation risk.

Primary Offender Motivations

Motivation Type	Description	Investigation Priority
Opportunistic	Crime of chance with minimal planning	Immediate area sweep
Grooming-based	Relationship built over time	Social and digital analysis
Targeted	Victim selected in advance	Review known associates
Situational escalation	Conflict, coercion, or panic-driven	Focus on last-seen witnesses
Criminal enterprise	Trafficking, extortion, organized crime	Activate specialized units

Operational Insight: Motivation determines geography, concealment strategy, and speed of escalation.

2. Opportunity Zones

Opportunity zones are environments where offenders perceive low risk, high control, and reliable escape routes.

Common Opportunity Zones

Zone Type	Characteristics	Search Implication
Transitional spaces	Parking lots, stairwells, bus stops	Immediate CCTV review
Familiar routes	Daily commute or habitual paths	Reconstruct routines
Low-visibility areas	Alleys, vacant lots, underpasses	Ground search priority
Social environments	Schools, gyms, cafés	Witness canvassing
Digital spaces	Social media, gaming platforms	Grooming detection

Professional Insight: Most abductions occur within 1–3 km of the victim's routine movement—not in remote locations.

3. Grooming Signals — Pre-Abduction Indicators

A significant number of abductions, particularly involving minors and vulnerable adults, are preceded by grooming behaviors both offline and online.

Behavioral Grooming Signals

Signal	Description	Required Action
Sudden secrecy	Hidden chats, unexplained contacts	Immediate digital review
Gifts or favors	Money, rides, devices	Identify source
Emotional dependency	Exclusivity statements	Interview social circle
Boundary testing	Gradual rule violations	Escalate risk
Isolation tactics	Discouraging family contact	High-priority alert

Digital Grooming Indicators

Indicator	Platform Examples	Evidence to Preserve
Alternate accounts	Instagram, Snap chat, Discord	Usernames, timestamps
Migration to private apps	Telegram, Signal	Chat backups
Deleted conversations	Messaging platforms	Cloud and device backups
Gaming-based contact	Multiplayer games	Game IDs, logs

Critical Note: Grooming evidence is often deleted quickly. Preservation must occur immediately.

4. Geographic Clustering

Offenders typically operate within personal comfort zones where they feel anonymous and in control.

Types of Geographic Clusters

Cluster Type	Description	Search Strategy
Anchor points	Offender residence or workplace	Radius expansion
Transit corridors	Highways, rail lines, bus routes	Transport record analysis
Repeat locations	Same park, venue, or street	Historical crime review
Boundary zones	Jurisdictional overlaps	Multi-agency coordination

Key Insight: Offenders choose invisibility over boldness when selecting locations.

5. Time-Based Abduction Patterns

Temporal factors influence offender behavior and witness availability.

Time Window	Risk Profile	Response Priority
Early morning	Predictable routines, low witnesses	Rapid CCTV review
Afternoon	School transitions, crowds	Immediate alerts
Evening	Reduced visibility	Area containment
Late night	Sparse witnesses	Transport monitoring

6. Crime Pattern Blueprint — Operational Tool

This blueprint enables rapid, objective abduction assessment.

A. Abduction Pattern Assessment Table

Risk Level (Low / Medium / High)	Factor	Observation	Notes
	Victim vulnerability	Age, disability, mental state	
	LKP characteristics	Isolated or public	
	Grooming indicators	Present or absent	
	Witness availability	High or low	
	Digital anomalies	Yes or no	
	Geographic clustering	Known or unknown	

B. Immediate Abduction Response Checklist

Step	Action	Responsible Party
Secure LKP	Preserve scene and CCTV	Police / SPOC
Identify opportunity zones	1–3 km radius	Field teams
Preserve digital evidence	Devices and accounts	Technical lead
Interview witnesses	Structured questioning	Investigator
Escalate to higher agencies	If indicators present	Police liaison
Update Master Case File	Real-time documentation	SPOC

7. Distinguishing Abduction from Voluntary Disappearance

Indicator	Voluntary Disappearance	Abduction
Personal items left	Sometimes	Frequently
Digital silence	Planned	Sudden
Financial access	Controlled	Interrupted
Witness anomalies	Rare	Common
Signs of struggle	Absent	Possible

Professional Insight: In abduction cases, time directly correlates with survivability.

8. Integration with Other Chapters

Chapter	Contribution
Chapter 4 — LKP	Identifies opportunity zones and escape paths
Chapter 9 — Social Circles	Detects grooming and coercion
Chapter 10 — Digital Footprint	Preserves offender contact trails
Chapter 12 — Suicide vs. Staged	Prevents misclassification

Criminal abduction analysis must never occur in isolation.

9. Professional Warnings

- Avoid public accusations without evidence
- Do not conduct independent confrontations
- Preserve evidence exactly as found
- Coordinate all findings with law enforcement

Operational errors can endanger the victim and compromise prosecution.

10. Summary

Criminal abductions follow recognizable patterns rather than randomness. Opportunity zones, grooming indicators, geographic clustering, and temporal factors provide early detection leverage.

Structured analysis accelerates law enforcement escalation and effective resource deployment. The Crime Pattern Blueprint converts fear into focused investigative action.

Professional Insight: The faster the pattern is recognized, the sooner the crime can be interrupted.

13. Reading Behavior before the Disappearance

Recognizing Early Clues That Precede Vanishing

Most disappearances are preceded by subtle but observable changes in behavior. Friends, family members, and colleagues often notice these shifts but dismiss them as temporary stress or mood fluctuations. Systematic observation and structured recording of these signals can materially alter outcomes—supporting early intervention, accurate classification, and faster recovery.

This chapter provides practical tools to identify, document, and integrate pre-incident behavioral indicators into an active investigation.

1. Language Shifts

Language reflects intent, emotional state, and planning. Changes in speech or writing frequently precede disappearance.

Key Language Indicators

Indicator	Description	Required Action
Change in tone	Sudden pessimism, detachment, hostility	Document exact phrases verbatim
Avoidance of future references	Stops discussing upcoming plans or events	Cross-check calendars and commitments
Repeated farewell phrases	Statements such as "You'll be fine without me"	Initiate immediate risk scoring
Ambiguous responses	Avoids specifics when questioned	Correlate with social and digital data
Online writing changes	Altered vocabulary, posting times, or themes	Preserve posts and metadata

Professional Tip: Track language changes over a minimum of 2–4 weeks. Use time stamped notes to identify patterns rather than isolated remarks.

2. Asset Liquidation

Financial and property behavior often signals pre-departure planning, distress, or coercion.

Signs of Pre-Disappearance Asset Activity

Behavior	Description	Investigative Notes
Selling valuables	Electronics, jewelry, vehicles	Cross-check sales platforms and receipts
Large withdrawals	Banks, digital wallets, crypto currency	Record amounts and timing
Account closures	Financial, subscription, or social accounts	Timestamp and sequence activity
Redistribution of assets	Unexpected gifts to friends or family	Verify recipients and context
Unusual bill payments	Prepaying rent, insurance, or loans	Identify forward planning

Professional Insight: Asset liquidation may indicate voluntary escape, financial collapse, or increased abduction risk. Context determines interpretation.

3. Withdrawal Patterns

Withdrawal across social, emotional, or routine domains is a key early warning signal.

Observable Withdrawal Types

Withdrawal Type	Examples	Recommended Action
Social	Cancels meetings, avoids gatherings	Interview social circle
Emotional	Reduced sharing, emotional flatness	Monitor closely and document
Digital	Stops messaging or posting	Review digital footprint
Work / School	Skipped responsibilities or attendance	Notify supervisors if high risk
Physical	Isolation, abandoned routines	Record in Master Case File

Professional Tip: Withdrawal combined with language shifts or asset activity significantly elevates risk classification.

4. Pre-Incident Signal Checklist

Use this checklist to log and score early indicators consistently.

Risk Level (Low / Medium / High)	Category	Signal	Observation	Notes / Date Recorded
	Language	Farewell hints or ambiguity		
	Language	Negative or detached tone		
	Financial	Unexplained withdrawals		
	Financial	Sale of valuables		
	Social	Avoidance of family or friends		
	Digital	Inactivity or account deletion		
	Routine	Cancelled commitments		
	Emotional	Mood swings, depression		
	Travel	Sudden bookings or inquiries		
	Environment	Changes to room, home, or workspace		

Usage Guidance

- Assign a risk level to each observed signal
- Update entries daily or weekly to detect escalation
- Include checklist in the Master Case File (Chapter 5)

- Combine with Behavioral Predictors (Chapter 11) for composite risk assessment

5. Integrating Signals with Investigation

Pre-incident signals gain predictive value when integrated with other intelligence streams.

Intelligence Source	Integration Purpose
LKP Analysis (Ch. 4)	Predict movement radius and likely last-seen zones
Social Circle Intelligence (Ch. 9)	Validate observations and timelines
Digital Footprint (Ch. 10)	Correlate online and offline withdrawal
Suicide vs. Staged Assessment (Ch. 12)	Determine urgency and life risk

Professional Insight: Early behavioral integration often enables intervention before disappearance or accelerates recovery timelines.

6. Operational Guidance

- **Daily monitoring:** Maintain a structured behavioral log
- **Pattern mapping:** Highlight converging changes across domains
- **Immediate escalation:** Notify authorities or mental health professionals if multiple high-risk signals align
- **Coordination:** Share updates with investigators via the Master Case File
- **Review cadence:** Reassess risk weekly or upon any major change

7. Summary

Indicators of disappearance frequently emerge well before the individual vanishes. Language shifts, asset activity, and withdrawal patterns are among the most reliable pre-incident signals.

Structured observation and documentation allow families and investigators to intervene earlier, allocate resources more effectively, and reduce harm.

Professional Insight: Systematic behavioral observation transforms hindsight into foresight—providing critical lead time when it matters most.

14. Victimology

Investigate the Person to Find the Path

Understanding the missing person as an individual—rather than a data point—is the cornerstone of effective investigation. Victimology is not about assigning blame. It is the disciplined analysis of personality, routines, vulnerabilities, and social context to predict behavior, identify risk zones, and narrow search focus.

When applied correctly, victimology transforms broad, reactive searches into targeted, intelligence-driven operations.

1. Core Principles of Victimology

- **Behavior drives location:** Daily habits, travel routines, and social patterns strongly influence last-known points and likely movement paths.
- **Vulnerabilities inform risk:** Age, health, finances, relationships, and psychological state shape urgency and harm probability.
- **Integration is critical:** Victimology is most effective when combined with Digital Footprints (Chapter 10), Pre-Incident Behavior (Chapter 14), and Abduction Pattern Analysis (Chapter 13).

Professional Insight: The more precise the victim profile, the narrower, faster, and more efficient the search becomes.

2. Victim Profiling Dimensions

A complete victimology profile examines the following ten dimensions:

Dimension	Focus Area	Example Indicators	Investigative Use
Demographics	Age, gender, occupation	Child, student, working adult	Risk assessment, LKP modeling
Personality	Risk tolerance, introversion/ extroversion	Withdrawn, impulsive	Voluntary disappearance likelihood
Habits & Routines	Daily schedule, hobbies	Gym visits, school route	Search radius mapping
Social Circles	Friends, family, peers	Close confidants, online groups	Interview prioritization
Mental Health	Stress, anxiety, depression	Therapy history, mood shifts	Suicide risk, escape probability
Financial Status	Assets, debts, access	ATM use, prepaid cards	Detect voluntary movement
Travel & Mobility	Transport preferences	Car, bicycle, public transit	Movement modeling
Digital Behavior	Online activity patterns	Apps, forums, DMs	OSINT integration
Vulnerabilities	Medical or physical conditions	Medication dependence	Urgency determination
Past Incidents	Prior disappearances or threats	Runaway behavior	Pattern prediction

3. Professional Victim Profiling Grid

This operational grid consolidates victim data and supports prioritization of search and investigative strategy.

Observed Data	Risk Level (Low / Medium / High)	Profile Category	Notes / Evidence	Priority Actions
Age 16, student	High	Demographics	School records verified	Focus LKP near school and commute
Introverted, cautious	Medium	Personality	Diary entries indicate stress	Expand social circle interviews
Daily jogging, library visits	Medium	Habits & Routines	Witness confirmations	Map routine routes
Best friend, uncle, gaming peers	Medium	Social Circles	Contact list compiled	Interview and cross-check
Mild anxiety	Medium	Mental Health	Pre-incident checklist	Monitor escalation
Limited funds, prepaid card	Low	Financial	Bank statements reviewed	Track withdrawals
Bicycle and bus use	Medium	Travel & Mobility	Transit data	Define movement radius
Active on Instagram, Discord	Medium	Digital Behavior	Messages preserved	OSINT and forensic review
Asthma,	High	Vulnerabilities	Medical	Emergency

peanut allergy			records	response prep
No prior incidents	Low	Past Behavior	Family confirmation	Establish baseline

Usage: Update this grid daily or as new intelligence emerges. Link all entries to the Master Case File (Chapter 5).

4. Integrating Victimology with Investigation

Victimology gains predictive power when integrated across intelligence domains:

Integration Area	Application
Risk Mapping	Combine profile with opportunity zones (Ch. 13)
Behavioral Signals	Refine urgency using pre-incident indicators (Ch. 14)
Digital Footprints	Overlay online behavior for movement prediction (Ch. 10)
Social Intelligence	Validate routines and vulnerabilities (Ch. 9)
Field Operations	Allocate resources by risk and probability zones

5. Operational Guidance for Investigators

- **Centralize data:** Store all victim information in a single Master Case File
- **Prioritize high-risk categories:** Age, medical needs, psychological distress, digital silence
- **Cross-check sources:** Triangulate family input, social data, digital logs, and field evidence
- **Update continuously:** Profiles evolve in voluntary disappearances or under coercion
- **Document rigorously:** Timestamp every interview,

observation, and record

6. Pre-Search Analytical Flow

1. Compile victim profile using the profiling grid
2. Map routine locations and determine probable LKP
3. Overlay geographic, behavioral, and psychological risk zones
4. Cross-reference digital footprint and social circle data
5. Adjust search strategy based on highest-priority indicators

Professional Insight: Victimology is dynamic. Continuous refinement converts reactive searching into predictive operations.

7. Summary

Victimology provides a 360-degree understanding of the missing person, enabling focused, strategic investigation rather than assumption-based searching.

Structured profiling grids consolidate demographics, routines, social connections, vulnerabilities, and digital behavior into actionable intelligence. When integrated with behavioral analysis, digital evidence, and abduction pattern recognition, victimology significantly increases the probability of rapid recovery.

Professional Insight: Investigate the person to find the path. Every habit, relationship, and vulnerability is a clue within the larger disappearance puzzle.

15. Surveillance Techniques

Ethical and Legal Observation Methods

Surveillance is one of the most powerful tools in missing-person investigations, but it must be conducted legally, ethically, and systematically. Improper surveillance can compromise evidence, violate privacy laws, expose observers to danger, and undermine prosecutions.

This chapter outlines professional-grade static and mobile surveillance techniques, pattern logging, and structured documentation designed to support lawful intelligence gathering.

1. Core Principles of Surveillance

- **Legality first:** Never violate privacy, trespass, or unlawfully intercept communications. Operate only within local law and authorization.
- **Ethical observation:** Surveillance is objective, non-intrusive information gathering—not harassment or intimidation.
- **Consistency over intensity:** Surveillance succeeds through structured timing, repetition, and logging.
- **Safety priority:** Observers must never confront subjects or suspected offenders.

Professional Insight: Surveillance gathers intelligence—it does not resolve situations through direct action.

2. Static Surveillance (Fixed Observation)

Static surveillance involves monitoring a fixed location to document movement, interactions, and environmental patterns.

Common Applications

- Residences, workplaces, or habitual locations
- Areas surrounding the Last Known Point (LKP)
- Locations identified through victim routines or opportunity zones

Operational Guidelines

Step	Description	Notes
Location selection	Choose concealed vantage points	Vehicles, windows, rooftops
Equipment	Binoculars, cameras, notebooks, timers	Recording only if legal
Observation schedule	Continuous or shift-based	Rotate observers
Behavior logging	Arrivals, departures, interactions	Use standardized logs
Contingency planning	Exit routes and safety plans	Mandatory in urban areas

Professional Tip: Static surveillance is most effective in predictable, high-probability locations.

3. Mobile Surveillance (Follow-Based Observation)

Mobile surveillance tracks subject movement without engagement. It requires planning, discipline, and coordination.

Core Principles

Principle	Description
Distance management	Maintain non-detectable spacing
Route awareness	Know alternate routes and exits
Observer teams	Multiple personnel for redundancy
Communication	Discrete, secure messaging
Documentation	Continuous lawful note-taking

Professional Tip: Mobile surveillance is most effective in urban or fluid environments where routines are disrupted.

4. Pattern Logging

Pattern logging converts observation into actionable intelligence.

Key Elements to Track

- Arrival and departure times
- Vehicles, license plates, and identifiers
- Interactions with known or unknown individuals
- Route repetition or deviation
- Behavioral anomalies

Intelligence Value

- Reveals habitual routines
- Anticipates future movement
- Identifies risk escalation or abduction indicators

5. Surveillance Log Template

Use the following standardized template for all observation activities:

Date	Time	Location / Coordinates	Subject Observed	Behavior Notes	Vehicle / Identifier	Duration	Action / Follow-Up

Instructions for Use

- Record observations immediately—never rely on memory
- Use precise timestamps (24-hour format)
- Include full identifiers when possible
- Document anomalies, not just routine behavior
- Upload logs to the Master Case File daily

6. Integration with Other Investigative Tools

Intelligence Source	Surveillance Application
LKP Analysis (Ch. 4)	Select observation zones
Victimology (Ch. 15)	Predict timing and locations
Digital Footprint (Ch. 10)	Anticipate movement windows
Pre-Incident Behavior (Ch. 14)	Detect voluntary or high-risk shifts
Abduction Patterns (Ch. 13)	Identify opportunity zones

Professional Insight: Surveillance is most effective when guided by behavioral and geographic intelligence.

7. Professional Guidelines

- Remain unobtrusive and avoid detection
- Rotate observers to prevent fatigue and pattern exposure
- Coordinate with law enforcement for elevated-risk operations
- Document environmental context (weather, crowds, lighting)

- Review logs daily for pattern recognition

8. Summary

Surveillance is a foundational investigative tool for tracking and predicting movement in missing-person cases. Static surveillance excels in predictable environments, while mobile surveillance supports dynamic tracking.

Structured pattern logging transforms raw observation into intelligence. When integrated with victimology, LKP analysis, digital footprints, and behavioral indicators, surveillance becomes a precision instrument rather than passive watching.

Professional Insight: Ethical, legal, and disciplined surveillance protects the investigation, the observer, and—ultimately—the missing person.

16. Financial Forensics

Money Almost Always Leaves a Trail

In missing-person investigations, financial activity is **behavior made observable**.

Every withdrawal, transfer, payment, or financial silence provides insight into **intent, timing, direction, and survivability**.

This chapter establishes a **legal, ethical, and systematic framework** for analyzing financial data to reconstruct movement, assess risk, and identify third-party involvement.

1. Why Financial Forensics Is Critical

Financial data can answer questions that witnesses often cannot.

Key Investigative Questions Answered by Financial Analysis

Question	Financial Indicator
Planned vs impulsive disappearance	Pre-withdrawals, asset liquidation
Independent survival vs coercion	Spending consistency and access
Third-party control	Geographic or behavioral anomalies
Post-disappearance location	ATM, POS, or digital transaction data

Professional Insight:

A single ATM transaction can reduce a **20-km search radius to under 200 meters** when time and location are analyzed together.

2. Financial Behavior After Disappearance — Interpretive Matrix

Financial Signal	Likely Interpretation	Risk Level
Sudden large cash withdrawals	Planned movement or escape	Medium–High
No financial activity	Incapacitation, detention, or death	High
Small, repeated withdrawals	Survival mode	Medium
Transfers to unknown accounts	Coercion or pre-planning	High
Crypto liquidation	Identity reinvention or flight	Medium
Spending inconsistent with habits	External influence	High

3. ATM Mapping (High-Value Tool)

ATM transactions provide **time + location + intent**.

3.1 ATM Mapping Procedure (Checklist)

Step	Action	Notes
1	Obtain bank statements (90–180 days)	Include all known accounts
2	Identify ATM ID, date, time, amount	Exact timestamps required
3	Cross-reference CCTV availability	Bank, retail, street cameras
4	Identify nearby transit nodes	Bus, rail, taxi stands
5	Overlay with LKP (Ch. 4)	Confirm movement direction
6	Overlay victim routines (Ch. 15)	Detect deviations

3.2 ATM Pattern Indicators

Pattern	Interpretation	Priority Action
ATM near highway	Long-distance movement	Expand radius
ATM near hospital	Injury or distress	Hospital canvass
ATM near transit hub	Transit phase	Ticketing review
Repeated ATM use (same area)	Temporary shelter or hiding	Ground search

4. Transaction Timing Analysis

Timing is often more probative than amount.

Timing Pattern	Interpretation
Night-time withdrawals	Avoidance behavior
Immediate post-disappearance use	Panic or pre-planning
Withdrawals aligned with paydays	Routine-driven
Irregular timing	Stress, coercion, or surveillance avoidance

Professional Rule:

Always analyze **time and location together**. Either alone is insufficient.

5. Hidden Accounts & Financial Blind Spots

Families often provide only primary accounts. Investigators must assume **secondary financial identities exist**.

5.1 Commonly Missed Financial Assets

Asset Type	Detection Method
Secondary bank accounts	KYC / identity-linked search
Prepaid debit cards	Receipts, emails, packaging
Digital wallets	App audit, SMS alerts
Employer salary accounts	HR verification
Investment / trading apps	Phone app inventory
Loan or credit accounts	Credit bureau inquiry

5.2 Behavioral Indicators of Hidden Accounts

Indicator	Investigative Meaning
Unexplained cash flow pre-disappearance	Financial staging
Deleted or suppressed alerts	Concealment
Financial secrecy with family	Parallel accounts
Multiple phone numbers	Account compartmentalization

6. Crypto currency Tracing (Restricted Domain)

Crypto currency is frequently used for **anonymity, cross-border movement, and asset concealment.**

6.1 Crypto Entry Points

Source	Evidence
Phone apps	Wallets, exchanges
Emails	Exchange confirmations
SMS	OTPs, alerts
Browser history	Wallet access
Notebooks	Seed phrases

6.2 Crypto Activity Interpretation

Crypto Behavior	Likely Meaning	Risk
Stable coin conversion	Long-term planning	Medium
Rapid liquidation	Urgency or fear	High
Dormant wallet	Loss of access or control	High
New wallet creation	Identity reset	Medium

Critical Note:

Crypto tracing typically requires **law enforcement or court authorization**. Families should **document only**, never attempt access.

7. Third-Party Financial Access (Red-Flag Zone)

Use of funds without the individual's control significantly escalates risk.

Indicators of Unauthorized Access

Indicator	Risk Level	Required Action
ATM use without phone movement	High	Immediate police escalation
Transactions after confirmed incapacitation	High	Bank + law enforcement
Geographic mismatch	High	Treat as coercion
PIN reset attempts	High	Account lockdown

Scenario Risk Matrix

Scenario	Risk Level
Family member accessing funds	Medium
Unknown third party	High
Criminal network involvement	Critical

8. Financial Forensics Log (Master Template)

Mandatory for all investigations

Date	Time	Transaction Type	Amount	Location / Platform	Linked Evidence	Interpretation	Acti
		ATM / Card / Transfer / Crypto			CCTV / Email / Receipt		

Instructions

- Log transactions **chronologically**
- Use **exact timestamps**
- Attach **verifiable evidence**
- Update daily and sync with the **Master Case File (Ch. 5)**

Professional Insight (Closing)

Money rarely disappears by accident.

When analyzed with **discipline, legality, and behavioral context**, financial data becomes one of the **fastest and most reliable tools** for reconstructing movement, detecting coercion, and prioritizing search and rescue efforts.

17. Cell Phone Intelligence

Understanding What Telecom Data Reveals

Cell phones are **real-world digital beacons.**

Every call, message, data session, or tower connection creates a **time-stamped, location-linked record** that can confirm movement, identify last-known positions, and reveal abnormal behavior.

Professional Insight:

A single verified tower ping can redirect search teams and save critical hours.

1. Core Principles of Cell Phone Intelligence

Principle	Operational Meaning
Legality & Authorization	Only authorized agencies may request official CDR or tower data
Integration	Telecom data must be analyzed alongside victimology, LKP, and financial activity
Pattern Analysis	Gaps, anomalies, and frequency matter more than raw volume
Cross-Verification	Validate findings with CCTV, financial logs, and witness data
Documentation	All interpretations must be logged and time-stamped

2. Call Detail Record (CDR) Analysis

CDRs contain **metadata only**—not content—but are extremely powerful.

2.1 Core CDR Elements & Investigative Use

CDR Element	Description	Investigative Value
Caller / Receiver ID	Numbers contacted	Identify networks & grooming
Timestamp	Exact date and time	Reconstruct timeline
Duration	Length of interaction	Engagement intensity
Tower ID	Cell site used	Approximate location
Call Type	Voice / SMS / data	Prioritize communication
Roaming Info	Network changes	Detect regional movement

2.2 CDR Analysis Workflow (Checklist)

Step	Action	Notes
1	Request CDR legally	Law enforcement only
2	Sort chronologically	Include all call types
3	Identify new or frequent contacts	Compare with known circle
4	Map tower IDs	Convert to coordinates
5	Flag anomalies	Time, frequency, silence
6	Cross-check	Digital, financial, CCTV

3. Cell Tower Triangulation

Triangulation estimates location using multiple tower connections.

3.1 Triangulation Method

Step	Description
Identify ≥3 tower IDs	Sequential or overlapping connections
Map coverage radius	Based on carrier data
Plot intersection zones	Approximate device location
Adjust for variables	Terrain, signal strength, congestion

Professional Insight:

In dense urban areas, triangulation can reduce search zones from **kilometers to hundreds of meters.**

4. Dead Zones & Signal Gaps

Dead zones occur when a phone cannot connect to towers.

Investigative Meaning of Signal Gaps

Scenario	Interpretation	Action
Sudden silence after movement	Device powered off or seized	Immediate ground search
Silence in known dead zone	Terrain or infrastructure	Map entry/exit points
Silence after threatening contact	High-risk escalation	Treat as critical

Operational Tips

- Use carrier coverage maps
- Cross-reference with terrain (tunnels, mountains, dense buildings)
- Treat **last ping before silence** as a high-priority anchor

5. Movement & Behavioral Indicators

Telecom data reveals **behavior**, not just location.

Pattern	Likely Interpretation
Frequent short calls	Anxiety, urgency
Rapid tower hopping	Transit or flight
Late-night pings	Avoidance or abduction
Sudden inactivity	Power loss, seizure, or harm
New SIM activation	Identity reset or staging
Cross-border roaming	Escalated movement risk

6. Cell Phone Intelligence Blueprint

A. Telecom Analysis Log (Master Table)

Timestamp	Tower ID	Coordinates	Call/ SMS/ Data	Duration	Observed Pattern	Interpretatio

Instructions

- Log sequentially
- Highlight deviations from normal routines
- Attach corroborating evidence where available
- Update daily in the **Master Case File (Ch. 5)**

B. Operational Flow Checklist

Phase	Action
Authorization	Obtain legal access to CDR
Organization	Sort data chronologically
Mapping	Convert tower IDs to geography
Triangulation	Narrow probable zones
Gap Analysis	Identify dead zones & silence
Behavioral Review	Detect anomalies
Integration	Cross-check with Ch. 4, 15, 17
Update Case File	Maintain live intelligence

7. Key Operational Considerations

Factor	Impact
Tower accuracy	Approximate, not GPS-exact
Device status	Power-off, airplane mode, SIM swap
Privacy laws	Violations invalidate evidence
Coordination	Telecom data must align with field ops

8. Summary

- Cell phones function as **continuous location and behavior sensors**
- CDR analysis, tower triangulation, and dead-zone mapping rapidly narrow search areas
- Behavioral anomalies revealed through telecom data provide **predictive insight**
- Structured logging ensures telecom intelligence is **actionable, traceable, and defensible**

Professional Insight:

Every ping tells a story. Interpreted correctly, it turns uncertainty into focused action and hours into lives saved.

18. Transportation Tracking

Reconstructing Movement When the Trail Goes Cold

When a person disappears, **distance becomes the primary threat to recovery**.

Transportation tracking converts uncertainty into **directional intelligence**, allowing investigators to reconstruct routes, predict destinations, and narrow operational zones.

Modern movement is rarely invisible. Roads, rails, airports, toll systems, and fuel networks continuously generate **timestamps, locations, and transactional evidence.**

Professional Insight:

Movement leaves patterns. Patterns reveal intent.

1. Core Principles of Transportation Intelligence

Principle	**Operational Meaning**
Movement requires infrastructure	Roads, rail, air, and fuel systems leave records
Speed indicates intent	Fast = urgency or planning; slow = confusion or distress
Distance alters risk	5 km ≠ 500 km in survivability and response
Time alignment is mandatory	Transport data must align with phone, finance, CCTV
Single data points mislead	Routes are built from sequences, not events

2. Immediate Transportation Assessment (First Questions)

Investigators must rapidly establish **mobility capability**.

Transportation Capability Checklist

Question	Yes / No	Evidence Source
Access to private vehicle?		Keys, ownership records
Public transit card owned?		Wallet, app, account
Tickets booked (air/rail/bus)?		Email, apps, financial logs
Fuel purchases detected?		Card statements, CCTV
Toll crossings recorded?		Toll authority
Route searches online?		Browser history
Luggage missing?		Home inventory

Initial Directional Assessment

Scenario	Investigative Direction
No transport indicators	Tight LKP radius search
Public transit usage	Expand along transit corridors
Private vehicle	Route modeling + toll/fuel analysis
Air travel	Immediate multi-agency escalation

3. Air Travel Tracking (High-Speed Displacement)

Air travel can move a person beyond **regional search capacity within hours**.

3.1 Air Travel Data Sources

Source	Investigative Value
Airline booking records	Intent and destination
ID / passport scans	Boarding confirmation
Baggage check-in	Trip duration planning
Payment method	Link to financial forensics
Airport CCTV	Physical confirmation

3.2 Behavioral Indicators (Air Travel)

Indicator	Interpretation
One-way ticket	Possible voluntary disappearance
Last-minute booking	Panic or escape
No checked luggage	Short stay or deception
International departure	Identity reset risk

Escalation Rule:

Confirmed air travel requires **immediate jurisdictional expansion.**

4. Bus and Rail Networks (Moderate-Speed, High Anonymity)

Public transit is commonly used due to affordability and reduced scrutiny.

4.1 Key Transit Records

Source	What It Reveals
Ticket purchase logs	Destination
Smart card usage	Boarding location
Platform CCTV	Physical presence
Seat assignments	Witness potential

4.2 Transit Pattern Interpretation

Pattern	Likely Meaning
Random destination	Disorientation or distress
Travel toward familiar city	Seeking safety
Travel to unknown region	Avoidance or concealment

5. Toll Booth Intelligence (Vehicle Route Reconstruction)

Toll systems are among the **most precise movement witnesses.**

Why Toll Data Matters

Value	Outcome
Time stamped crossings	Direction & speed
Sequential tolls	Route reconstruction
Gaps in toll usage	Stops or deviations
Exit point prediction	Forward deployment

Toll Pattern Interpretation

Pattern	Interpretation
Sequential tolls	Continuous travel
Extended gap	Stop or detour
Sudden route change	Evasion behavior

Professional Insight:

Three toll records can reconstruct an entire highway journey.

6. Fuel Station Mapping

Fuel purchases act as **forced behavioral anchors.**

What Fuel Data Reveals

Indicator	Meaning
Fuel far from home	Strong movement intent
Small refill	Uncertain destination
Large refill	Long-distance planning
CCTV behavior	Emotional state, companions

Fuel data is especially powerful when aligned with **toll gaps or GPS loss.**

7. Private Vehicle Route Modeling

If a personal vehicle is involved, assume **high autonomy and expanded reach.**

Critical Vehicle Data Sources

Source	Investigative Use
GPS / infotainment logs	Exact route history
Parking receipts	Stop locations
Traffic cameras	Visual confirmation
Residential sightings	Shelter identification
Dashcam footage	Timeline validation

High-Risk Vehicle Signals

Signal	Interpretation	Risk
Vehicle abandoned	Distress or staging	High
Vehicle hidden	Intentional disappearance	High
Vehicle destroyed	Criminal involvement	Critical

8. Movement Reconstruction Model (Operational Framework)

Step-by-Step Process

Step	Action
1	Confirm departure from LKP
2	Identify first transport event
3	Build chronological chain (timestamps only)
4	Calculate reachable distance between events
5	Predict logical destinations (resources, contacts)
6	Deploy search **ahead**, not behind

Strategic Rule:

Investigations fail when teams search where the person *was*, not where they are *going*.

9. Transportation Movement Log (Master Template)

Mandatory for route reconstruction

Date	Time	Transport Type	Location	Evidence Source	Direction	Distance from LKP	Interpretation	Action
		Flight / Bus / Rail / Toll / Fuel		Ticket / CCTV / Financial				

Instructions

- Log events sequentially
- Never infer direction without evidence
- Cross-reference with Chapters 17 (Finance) and 18 (Cell

Phone)

- Update the **Master Case File** continuously

10. Summary

- Transportation tracking converts missing-person cases from static searches into **forward-moving operations**
- Air, rail, road, toll, and fuel systems create **independent, corroborative movement records**
- Speed, distance, and direction provide insight into **intent and risk**
- Structured logging and time-aligned analysis prevent false assumptions and wasted resources

Professional Insight:

When movement is understood, uncertainty collapses—and search teams regain control of time and distance.

19. Open Source Intelligence (OSINT)

Leveraging Public Digital Data for Investigations

Open Source Intelligence (OSINT) is the systematic collection and analysis of **publicly available digital information**. In missing-person investigations, OSINT frequently uncovers **hidden communications, movement indicators, associates, and intent** that are invisible to traditional field methods.

Professional Insight:

In many modern disappearances, the *first actionable lead appears online.*

1. Core Principles of OSINT

Principle	Operational Meaning
Legality & Ethics	Access only publicly available information; no hacking or impersonation
Cross-Validation	OSINT must be verified through telecom, finance, CCTV, or witnesses
Digital Footprint Awareness	Individuals leave traces across platforms, often unintentionally
Identity Linking	Usernames, images, language, and timing create cross-platform links
Documentation	Every finding must be captured, time stamped, and sourced

2. Username & Digital Identity Tracing

People frequently reuse usernames, aliases, or email prefixes across platforms.

2.1 Username Tracing Workflow (Checklist)

Step	Action	Notes
1	Collect all known usernames	Social, gaming, forums
2	Identify variations	Numbers, spelling changes
3	Search across platforms	Social, forums, marketplaces
4	Use username search engines	Namechk, KnowEm, Sherlock
5	Capture matching profiles	Screenshot + timestamp
6	Validate ownership	Language, photos, contacts

2.2 Username Validation Indicators

Indicator	Meaning
Similar posting style	Likely same individual
Shared profile images	Strong linkage
Overlapping contacts	Network confirmation
Consistent time-zone activity	Geographic alignment

Professional Insight:

Even small username variations often reveal **parallel or hidden accounts.**

3. Reverse Image Intelligence

Images often reveal **location, timing, identity, or staging**.

3.1 Reverse Image Search Procedure

Step	Action	Tools / Notes
1	Collect image	Original file preferred
2	Upload to reverse engines	Google, TinEye, Yandex
3	Review duplicates	Compare timestamps
4	Extract metadata (if present)	EXIF, geotags
5	Analyze visual clues	Signs, terrain, objects
6	Cross-check with case data	Transport, LKP, CDR

3.2 Image Intelligence Indicators

Indicator	Interpretation
Image reused elsewhere	Broader online presence
Background landmarks	Location inference
Image edited or staged	Possible deception
Metadata mismatch	Re-uploaded or concealed

Professional Note:

Even when metadata is removed, **visual context often reveals location.**

4. Forum, Community & Platform Tracking

Niche communities frequently contain **behavioral and relational intelligence.**

4.1 Forum Tracking Workflow

Step	Action	Notes
1	Identify relevant platforms	Reddit, Discord, hobby forums
2	Search for usernames/aliases	Internal search, Google dorks
3	Archive relevant posts	Screenshot or PDF
4	Analyze posting behavior	Timing, language, tone
5	Identify contacts & replies	Network mapping
6	Link to other platforms	Cross-identity tracing

4.2 Behavioral Clues in Forums

Pattern	Likely Meaning
Posting at odd hours	Stress, movement, or hiding
Sudden cessation of posts	Disappearance onset
Location hints in language	Regional presence
Requests for help or rides	Pre-movement signals

Professional Insight:

Anonymity hides identity—but **reveals networks.**

5. OSINT Toolkit (Operational Reference)

Tool / Method	Purpose	Example Use
Google Advanced Search	Filter by site, date	site:reddit.com username
Username search engines	Cross-platform tracing	Namechk, KnowEm
Reverse image engines	Image validation	TinEye, Yandex
Social platforms	Profile analysis	Instagram, TikTok, Discord
Metadata extractors	File intelligence	ExifTool, Fotoforensics
Archiving tools	Evidence preservation	Wayback, Archive.today
Geo location tools	Location inference	Google Earth, Street View
OSINT log sheet	Lead tracking	Link to Master Case File

Usage Protocol

- Screenshot **every finding**
- Record **URL, platform, date, and time**
- Avoid assumptions—label findings as *unverified* until corroborated
- Sync continuously with the **Master Case File**

6. OSINT Integration Matrix

Intelligence Stream	OSINT Contribution
Victimology (Ch. 15)	Validate habits, interests, contacts
Transportation (Ch. 19)	Detect route research, destination hints
Financial Forensics (Ch. 17)	Match online purchases or wallets
Cell Phone Intelligence (Ch. 18)	Correlate posting times with pings
Surveillance (Ch. 16)	Identify locations for monitoring

7. Common OSINT Errors (Avoidance Checklist)

Error	Consequence
Assuming similar usernames are identical	False attribution
Failing to document evidence	Unusable intelligence
Ignoring platform privacy settings	Missed data
Overlooking image background clues	Lost location leads
Not cross-checking findings	Misleading conclusions

Professional Reminder:

OSINT alone is suggestive. **OSINT integrated is decisive.**

8. OSINT Intelligence Log (Master Template)

Date	Platform	Username / ID	Content Type	URL / Source	Key Finding	Verification Status	Action
			Post / Image / Profile			Pending / Confirmed	

9. Summary

- OSINT extends investigations beyond physical terrain into the **digital environment**
- Username tracing, reverse image analysis, and forum monitoring uncover **hidden connections and movement clues**
- Structured tools and logs ensure findings are **traceable, ethical, and defensible**
- When integrated with victimology, transport tracking, financial data, cell phone intelligence, and surveillance, OSINT transforms scattered digital traces into **actionable investigative intelligence**

Core Insight:

The internet never forgets. OSINT teaches investigators how to read what it quietly remembers.

20. Organizing Civilian Search Parties

Turning Urgency Into Structured Action

Civilian volunteers bring speed, numbers, and local knowledge. Without structure, they also bring **risk, evidence loss, and confusion.**

A civilian search must operate as a **controlled field operation**, not a spontaneous crowd.

Professional Insight:

Chaos is the enemy of discovery. Structure multiplies search effectiveness.

1. Criteria for Civilian Search Deployment

1.1 When Civilian Searches ARE Appropriate

Condition	Status
Law enforcement approval or coordination	Required
Search zone clearly defined	Required
Immediate terrain coverage needed	Suitable
Time-sensitive survival factors	Suitable
Low likelihood of active crime scene	Suitable

1.2 When Civilian Searches Should NOT Begin

Condition	Risk
Active or suspected crime scene	Evidence destruction
Forensics not completed	Case compromise
Hazardous terrain	Volunteer injury
Severe weather conditions	Operational failure

Golden Rule:

Civilians support investigations — they **never replace professionals.**

2. Risks of Unstructured Searches

Operational Failure	Consequence
Evidence contamination	Loss of forensic value
Volunteers searching solo	Injury or secondary disappearance
Duplicate area coverage	Time and resource waste
No central communication	Missed discoveries
Emotion-driven decisions	Strategic collapse

3. Civilian Search Command Structure

Even small searches require leadership clarity.

3.1 Recommended Command Hierarchy

Role	Core Responsibility
Search Coordinator	Overall authority and strategy
Operations Lead	Assigns zones and teams
Safety Officer	Terrain, weather, medical oversight
Communications Officer	Field-to-command updates
Documentation Officer	Logs zones, findings, times
Volunteer Manager	Registration, briefing, accountability

Professional Insight:

One clear leader prevents ten conflicting decisions.

4. Pre-Search Operational Briefing (Mandatory)

4.1 Briefing Checklist

Topic	Covered (✓)
Missing person description	
Last Known Point (LKP)	
Assigned zones and boundaries	
Safety rules	
Communication protocol	
Reportable findings	
Search end time	

4.2 Volunteer Registration Log

Name	Contact	Arrival Time	Team	Zone	Check-Out Time

Why this matters:

If you don't know who is in the field, you cannot ensure everyone returns.

5. Search Zone Definition

5.1 Zone Design Principles (Checklist)

- Start at LKP and expand outward
- Prioritize high-probability terrain:
  - Water bodies
  - Wooded areas
  - Abandoned structures
  - Transit corridors
- Complete zones fully before expanding

Strategic Rule:

Search thoroughly before searching widely.

6. Volunteer Deployment Map (Operational Template)

Zone ID	Terrain Type	Priority	Team Assigned	Start Time	End Time	Findings	Re-Search
A	Residential	High	Team 1				
B	Parkland	High	Team 2				
C	Commercial	Medium	Team 3				
D	Peripheral Roads	Medium	Team 4				
E	Extended Radius	Low	Team 5				

Deployment Rules

- Minimum **two volunteers per team**
- Maintain visual or communication contact
- Zones cleared **only after documentation**

7. Search Team Structure

Role	Responsibility
Team Leader	Navigation, decisions, reporting
Navigator	Tracks coverage area
Observer	Visual scanning
Recorder	Logs findings and time

Optional Enhancements (Large Searches):

- Drone units

- Canine teams
- Medical support

8. Field Search Protocol

8.1 Volunteers MUST

Action	Purpose
Move slowly	Avoid missing clues
Scan ground and surroundings	Detect evidence
Report immediately	Preserve timeline

Look For:

- Clothing or footwear
- Personal items
- Disturbed ground
- Footprints
- Signs of shelter

8.2 Volunteers MUST NOT

Prohibited Action	Reason
Touch evidence	Destroys forensic value
Enter private property	Legal risk
Confront individuals	Safety risk
Move or collect clues	Evidence contamination

Professional Warning:

The moment evidence is touched, truth may be erased.

9. Communication Protocol

9.1 Primary Communication Methods (Choose One)

Method	Use Case
Radio	Large or remote areas
Messaging group	Urban or compact zones
Command phone	Centralized reporting

9.2 Standard Reporting Format

Location → Observation → Urgency

Example:

"Zone B, north trail junction. Backpack matching description located. No movement observed."

10. Safety Protocol (Non-Negotiable)

Hazard	Prevention
Heat / cold	Hydration, weather gear
Wildlife	Maintain distance
Rough terrain	Proper footwear
Darkness	Suspend search or add lighting
Emotional exhaustion	Rotate teams

Rule:

Set a hard stop time — exhausted volunteers make mistakes.

11. Field Documentation (Force Multiplier)

If it isn't logged, it didn't happen.

11.1 Field Search Log

Date	Team	Zone	Area Covered	Duration	Evidence Found	Escalated To	Notes

All records must be stored in the **Master Case File (Chapter 5)**.

12. Psychological Management of Volunteers

Volunteers are emotionally invested — leadership must manage morale without sacrificing discipline.

Leadership Guidelines

Action	Purpose
Calm communication	Prevent panic
No speculation	Avoid misinformation
Realistic expectations	Maintain trust
Visible gratitude	Sustain engagement
Team rotation	Prevent burnout

Insight:

> Hope motivates — discipline saves lives.

13. Pause vs. Escalation Criteria

Pause the Search If:

Condition
Severe weather
Unsafe terrain
Law enforcement request
Evidence discovered

Escalate the Search If:

Trigger
Multiple clues emerge
Survival probability shifts
New intelligence changes radius

14. Common Leadership Failures (Avoid)

Error	Impact
Uncontrolled volunteer arrival	Chaos
Expanding too quickly	Missed evidence
Ignoring documentation	Lost intelligence
Overlooking safety	Injuries
No professional coordination	Case damage

Professional Insight:

A smaller, disciplined search outperforms a massive, disorganized one.

15. Strategic Value of Civilian Searches

Properly organized civilian searches can:

Benefit	Effect
Expand manpower	Faster coverage
Cover difficult terrain	Increased discovery
Generate community intelligence	New leads
Support professionals	Operational leverage

Summary

Civilian search parties are powerful **only when structured.**

- Establish command early
- Define zones clearly
- Deploy teams methodically
- Communicate precisely
- Document relentlessly
- Protect volunteer safety

Core Truth:
Searching is not about how many people you have — it is about how intelligently you deploy them.

21. Search Dogs, Drones, and Technology

Operational Checklist & Capability Matrix

Technology accelerates discovery **only when deployed deliberately**. This chapter provides a structured framework to select, deploy, and document advanced search tools without disrupting ground operations or evidence integrity.

1. Technology & Resource Deployment Matrix

1.1 Tool Capability & Operational Checklist

Tool / Resource	Optimal Deployment Window	Primary Use	Key Advantages	Key Limitations	Ma Op Che
Search & Rescue Dogs (Tracking Dogs)	First 24–72 hours	Follow freshest human scent	Rapid direction-of-travel detection	Scent contamination, weather sensitivity	✔ S unc scen Res foot Use han rout
Trailing Dogs	Movement suspected, route unclear	Track ground disturbance & human odor	Effective in semi-urban terrain	Reduced accuracy in crowds	✔ N prol ✔ D sect Mai com com
Cadaver Dogs	Suspected fatality / long-term case	Detect human remains	Detects decomposition odor	High emotional impact	✔ C clea Pre brie Pres indi
Thermal Drones	Night, forest, disaster zones	Detect heat signatures	Rapid wide-area coverage	Degraded in high ambient heat	✔ A auth Cer ✔ C ma Rec
High-Resolution	Open terrain, cliffs,	Visual identification	Clothing/ object	Weather & wind	✔ I flig

Camera Drones	coastlines		recognition	dependent	Batter redun Zoom
Ground Search Robots	Collapsed/ unsafe structures	Remote visual access	Protects human searchers	Cost, technical complexity	✓ Ris assess Train opera feed t comm
GPS Trackers *(pre-installed only)*	Kidnapping/ vulnerable persons	Real-time movement data	Immediate actionable intel	Requires prior installation	✓ Ac tracki ✓ No enforc Log c
Mobile Signal Detectors	Phone believed powered on	Narrow device location	Reduces search radius	Telecom coordination required	✓ Tel liaisor Triang setup
Underwater Sonar	Water involvement suspected	Detect submerged objects	High accuracy	Specialist equipment only	✓ Ma deploy Grid Sonar docun

2. Capability Matrix — Matching Tool to Scenario

Scenario	Recommended Tool(s)	Operational Rationale
Lost child in forest	Thermal drone + tracking dogs	Speed + scent accuracy
Elderly person with dementia	Trailing dogs + grid search	Predictable wandering behavior
Suspected kidnapping	GPS + cell phone intelligence	Time-critical tracking
Mountain or cliff disappearance	Camera drone	Safe aerial visibility
Disaster rubble	Ground robots + cadaver dogs	Access + detection
Vehicle/body suspected in water	Sonar	Only reliable detection method

3. Technology Deployment Decision Checklist

Decision Question	If YES	If NO
Is survival time critical?	Deploy drones immediately	Begin structured ground search
Is terrain unsafe for humans?	Use robots or aerial assets	Assign trained ground teams
Is there a digital trail?	Activate telecom & financial analysis	Focus on physical search
Are weather conditions stable?	Launch aerial operations	Delay air assets, reinforce ground
Is law enforcement informed?	Coordinate jointly	Notify before deployment

4. Integrated Technology Deployment Workflow

Phase	Action
Assessment	Match tool to terrain, time, and risk
Authorization	Confirm legal & aviation permissions
Deployment	Assign certified operators only
Documentation	Log start time, grid, results
Integration	Feed results into Master Case File
Review	Adjust strategy based on findings

5. Golden Rules of Tech-Assisted Searches

Rule	Operational Value
Technology supports — never replaces — ground intelligence	Prevents false confidence
Always document deployment time & results	Legal defensibility
Avoid tool overload	Prevents command confusion
Match tool to terrain, not trend	Strategy over novelty
Centralize all outputs in command log	Prevents data fragmentation

6. Summary (Operational Takeaway)

Advanced tools dramatically **increase speed and coverage**, but only when:

- Deployed at the right time
- Matched to terrain and risk
- Operated by trained personnel
- Integrated into a single command structure

Core Operational Truth:
Technology does not find people —
disciplined deployment of technology does.

22. Wilderness vs. Urban Searches

Terrain Survival Probability & Operational Search Framework

Search strategy must shift immediately based on **terrain type**. Survival probability, evidence type, and movement behavior differ sharply between wilderness and urban environments. This chapter provides **decision matrices and predictive tables** to guide rapid, terrain-appropriate deployment.

1. Terrain Survival Probability Chart

Terrain Type	**Survival Probability (0–24 hrs)**	**24–72 Hours**	**Beyond 72 Hours**	**Primary Risks**	**Search Urgency Level**
Dense Forest / Jungle	High (if uninjured)	Moderate	Drops sharply	Exposure, dehydration, disorientation	**Extreme — deploy immediately**
Mountains / Cliffs	Moderate	Low	Very Low	Falls, hypothermia	**Extreme**
Desert / Arid Land	Moderate (if water present)	Very Low	Critical	Heatstroke, dehydration	**Immediate aerial search**
Coastal / Shoreline	Moderate	Low	Very Low	Tides, drowning	**Time-sensitive**
Urban City	High	Moderate	Case-dependent	Crime, concealment	**Intelligence-led search**
Abandoned Structures	Moderate	Low	Very Low	Injury, foul play	**High-priority sweep**
Cold Climate	Moderate	Very Low	Critical	Hypothermia	**Golden 24-hour window**

2. Wilderness vs. Urban — Operational Difference Matrix

Investigation Factor	Wilderness Search	Urban Search
Primary Strategy	Search the terrain	Search the network
Probability Pattern	Usually accidental	Often intentional or crime-linked
Movement Radius	Limited by fatigue & terrain	Expands rapidly via transport
Evidence Type	Footprints, broken vegetation	CCTV, digital records, witnesses
Best Tools	Dogs, drones, thermal imaging	Telecom data, financial trails
Command Style	Centralized field command	Intelligence coordination cell
Critical Skill	Grid discipline	Data synthesis

3. Rapid Terrain Classification Checklist

Assessment Question	If YES	Immediate Action
Person inexperienced outdoors?	Likely immobilized nearby	Start tight radius (1–3 km)
Weather changed recently?	Exposure risk increased	Deploy rescue teams rapidly
Known hiking / trekking route?	Predictable movement	Search forward along trail
Signs of voluntary disappearance?	Lower terrain risk	Shift to urban intelligence
Last phone ping near remote area?	Strong wilderness indicator	Launch aerial & dog teams

4. Survival Behavior Predictor Table

Missing Person Profile	Likely Behavior	Search Adjustment
Lost child	Keeps moving, may hide	Expand perimeter rapidly
Elderly / dementia	Walks until exhausted	Focus paths & downhill routes
Injured adult	Stops within short distance	Tight grid, slow pace
Experienced hiker	Seeks shelter and water	Check natural cover, water sources
Suicidal subject	Chooses isolation	Search hazard & remote zones first

5. The Golden Strategy Shift Rule

Time Since Disappearance	Strategic Priority
0–12 hours	Treat as **rescue mission**
12–24 hours	Aggressive area containment
24–48 hours	Combine search + investigation
48+ hours	Increase criminal probability
72+ hours	Transition toward forensic readiness

6. High-Risk Terrain Indicators

Indicator	Operational Significance
Steep drop-offs nearby	Victims often invisible from air
Water bodies within 2 km	Strong statistical pull factor
Sudden weather change	Disorientation and injury spike
Dense vegetation	Collapse without visibility
Animal territory	Shortens survival window

7. Command-Level Deployment Checklist

Priority Action	Execution Standard
Establish Incident Command Post	Within first operational hour
Divide terrain into grids	Prevent duplication
Assign sector leaders	Maintain accountability
Track searched vs. unsearched zones	Live operational map
Schedule re-searches	Many finds occur on second pass
Control volunteer flow	Chaos reduces detection probability

8. Expert Insight — Rule of Statistical Gravity

Environmental Factor	Behavioral Pull
Roads, trails, rivers	Humans gravitate toward paths
Sloped terrain	Disoriented persons move downhill
Water scarcity	Movement toward water sources
Panic response	Circular walking patterns common

Summary (Operational Doctrine)

Terrain dictates survival probability, evidence type, and movement behavior.

Searches fail when **urban logic is applied to wilderness**, or **terrain logic is applied to cities.**

Core Command Truth:

Do not ask *where the person disappeared —*

ask **what the environment will do to them next.**

23. Media Strategy

Using Public Attention to Accelerate Discovery (Without Compromising the Case)

Media exposure is an operational tool. Used correctly, it multiplies tip flow and awareness. Used incorrectly, it compromises evidence, alerts perpetrators, and endangers the missing person.

Core Doctrine:

Media is intelligence amplification — not emotional expression.

1. Core Principles of Media Engagement

Principle	Operational Rule	Enforcement Standard
Controlled Communication	Single authorized spokesperson only	No parallel statements
Accuracy Over Speed	Verify before release	No speculation
Information Containment	Limit sensitive details	Protect LKP & methods
Tip Amplification	Direct all responses to one channel	Centralized logging
Legal Compliance	Avoid prejudicial statements	Police/legal review

2. Media Engagement Timing Matrix

Situation	Media Action	Rationale
First 24 hours	Issue initial appeal	Public memory still fresh
Before police clearance	**Do not engage**	Prevent evidence compromise
Search area expands	Controlled update	Expand witness pool
Risk to public safety	Public alert	Prevent secondary harm
Minor / vulnerable adult	Immediate escalation	Higher recovery probability

3. Media Engagement Protocol (Checklist)

Step	Action	Responsible Role
1	Designate spokesperson	Family / Incident Command
2	Draft press release	Communications Officer
3	Legal & police review	Law enforcement / counsel
4	Release via approved outlets	Media liaison
5	Record all statements	Documentation officer
6	Monitor coverage & correct errors	Communications officer

4. Press Release Content Control Checklist

◈ Information Allowed for Release

Category	Approved Content
Identity	Name, age, physical description
Appearance	Clothing last seen wearing
Timing	Date & general time window
Location	**Generalized area only**
Safety	Medical needs (if critical)
Contact	Official tip line only

◈ Information Restricted

Restricted Detail	Risk Created
Exact LKP coordinates	Evidence compromise
Search tactics or zones	Offender evasion
Volunteer locations	Safety risk
Unverified sightings	Resource diversion
Personal routines	Exploitation risk

5. Press Release Template (Operational Standard)

Section	Required Content
Header	**Urgent Appeal: Missing Person — [Name]**
Identification	Name, age, height, weight, hair/eye color
Clothing	What they were last seen wearing
Last Known Circumstances	Brief, factual, non-speculative
Safety Concerns	Medical or vulnerability info (if applicable)
Public Request	"If you have information, contact..."
Instructions	"Do not intervene directly"
Official Contact	Police or designated command number

6. Social Media Deployment Matrix

Platform	Primary Use	Risk Control Measure
Facebook	Broad public reach	Moderate comments actively
Twitter / X	Rapid alerts & updates	Avoid LKP specifics
Instagram	Visual identification	Remove geotags
TikTok / Reels	Youth audience	No routine disclosure

Operational Rule:

All social posts must mirror the approved press release language.

7. Media Risk Mitigation Table

Common Error	Operational Consequence	Preventive Action
Unverified sightings shared	Wasted search resources	Internal verification first
Search zones disclosed	Evidence loss	Use generalized language
Emotional speculation	Public confusion	Stick to facts only
Too many media outlets	Message dilution	Prioritize key channels
Unmoderated comments	False leads	Assign moderation role

8. Media–Investigation Coordination Checklist

Requirement	Execution Standard
Drafts shared with police	Before publication
Tip intake centralized	Single phone/email
Tip log maintained	Linked to Master Case File
False leads filtered	Before field deployment
Media updates scheduled	Not reactive

9. Media as an Investigative Tool

Media Function	Investigative Value
Press coverage	Generates eyewitness tips
Social sharing	Surfaces digital sightings
Viral exposure	Reaches unknown witnesses
Journalist collaboration	Exposes criminal networks

10. Command-Level Rules (Non-Negotiable)

Rule	Reason
One voice only	Prevents contradictions
Facts over emotion	Preserves credibility
Document everything	Legal defensibility
Tips ≠ truth	Require verification
Silence is acceptable	When risk outweighs benefit

Summary — Operational Doctrine

Media is neither friend nor enemy — it is **leverage**.

Used correctly:

- It expands the witness pool
- Accelerates discovery
- Applies pressure where needed

Used poorly:

- It alerts perpetrators
- Destroys evidence
- Endangers lives

Core Command Truth:
Public attention must be **aimed**, not unleashed.

24. Partnering With Investigative Journalists

Amplifying Search Efforts without Compromising the Case

Investigative journalists can extend reach, uncover hidden networks, and generate actionable leads. When unmanaged, they can also expose tactics, alert offenders, or distort facts. This chapter defines a **controlled collaboration model** that protects the investigation while leveraging journalistic capability.

Operational Doctrine:

Journalists are force multipliers only when governed by rules, scope, and accountability.

1. Decision Matrix — When to Engage Investigative Journalists

Trigger Condition	Engagement Rationale	Authorization Level
Case stagnant > 48–72 hours	External pressure may unlock new leads	Incident Command
Child or vulnerable adult missing	Broader exposure increases recovery odds	Immediate
Suspected criminal involvement	Journalists may uncover concealed networks	Law enforcement review
Strong digital footprint	OSINT skills extend online reach	Communications lead
Limited official resources	Media supplements investigative capacity	Joint approval

2. Journalist Selection Criteria (Non-Negotiable)

Evaluation Factor	Acceptance Standard	Verification Method
Track record	Prior crime / missing-person investigations	Portfolio review
Credibility	Trusted by public & authorities	References
Confidentiality	Willing to honor embargoes	Written agreement
Reach	Access to relevant local / regional audience	Analytics
Analytical skill	Investigates beyond press releases	Past work review

Professional Rule:

If credibility is uncertain, do not engage — risk outweighs benefit.

3. Collaboration Blueprint (Operational Workflow)

Step	Action	Responsible Party	Control Measure
1	Identify vetted journalist(s)	Communications Officer	Credential check
2	Establish comms channel	Command + Journalist	Single point of contact
3	Define information scope	Incident Command	Public vs restricted
4	Share verified materials	Investigators	No speculation
5	Plan coverage schedule	Journalist + Spokesperson	Avoid saturation
6	Capture tips generated	Journalist → Command	Centralized logging
7	Review content pre-release	Command / Legal	Error correction
8	Post-event debrief	All parties	Strategy adjustment

4. Risk Mitigation Matrix

Risk	Operational Impact	Mitigation Control
Disclosure of search zones	Evidence loss / safety risk	Generalize locations
Misreporting	Public confusion	Pre-publication review
Perpetrator media monitoring	Evasion / evidence destruction	Delay sensitive details
Over-amplification	Volunteer chaos	Timed releases
Ethical breaches	Legal exposure	Vetted journalists only

5. Operational Integration with Investigation Streams

Investigation Area	Journalist Contribution	Command Control
OSINT & digital	Identify hidden accounts, aliases	Verification before action
Transport tracking	Validate public sightings	Cross-check timestamps
Witness discovery	Locate overlooked witnesses	Structured interviews
Media strategy	Align coverage with priorities	Command approval
Civilian mobilization	Controlled awareness	Avoid zone disclosure

6. Journalist Engagement Protocol (Checklist)

Phase	Responsible Party	Required Action	Timeline
Initial contact	Family / Comms Officer	Verify credentials	Day 2–3
Information sharing	Investigators	Provide verified facts only	< 24 hrs
Coverage planning	Journalist + Spokesperson	Agree on scope & timing	Day 3–4
Tip intake	Journalist	Forward all leads	Continuous
Verification	Search Coordinator	Triage & validate tips	Ongoing
Debrief	Command + Journalist	Assess impact	Weekly

7. Best-Practice Rules for Collaboration

Rule	Purpose
Single point of contact	Prevents message drift
Facts only, no theory	Preserves credibility
Protect LKP & tactics	Prevents offender advantage
Align releases with ops	Avoids interference
Log all media-generated tips	Maintains traceability

8. Command-Level Do's and Don'ts

DO

- Treat journalists as partners with boundaries
- Use written scopes and embargoes
- Integrate leads into the Master Case File
- Correct errors immediately

DO NOT

- Share investigative methods
- Allow unscheduled interviews
- Disclose volunteer locations
- React emotionally to coverage

9. Key Takeaways

Insight	Operational Meaning
Journalists extend reach	Use them strategically
Structure prevents harm	Rules protect the case
Tips require verification	Public input ≠ truth
Timing matters	Release information deliberately
Alignment is critical	Media must serve the search

Core Truth

Media is leverage.

Applied with discipline, it accelerates discovery.

Applied without control, it becomes an adversary.

25. Understanding the Law

Navigating Legal Structures in Missing Person Cases

A working knowledge of legal frameworks prevents investigative delays, protects evidence admissibility, and shields families and volunteers from unintended legal exposure.

Professional Insight:

Legal awareness turns families from passive observers into effective, protected partners in the search.

1. Legal Classification Matrix — Missing Person vs. Kidnapped

Classification	Legal Definition	Immediate Legal Effect	Priority Level
Missing Person	Whereabouts unknown; absence unexplained	Police file report, initiate search	Variable
Kidnapped / Abducted	Person taken unlawfully by force, threat, or coercion	Criminal investigation, warrants possible	High / Immediate

Common Misconceptions Clarified

Misconception	Reality	Operational Impact
All missing cases are criminal	Many are accidental or voluntary	Affects urgency
Family belief determines classification	Evidence determines classification	Police prioritization
Classification cannot change	It can escalate with new evidence	Case upgrade possible

Professional Insight:

Early identification of risk factors (minor, medical condition, prior threats) increases investigative priority.

2. Jurisdiction Determination Matrix

Factor	Investigative Effect	Responsible Authority
Location of disappearance	Primary jurisdiction	Local police
Suspected offender location	Secondary jurisdiction	Coordinating agency
Interstate movement	Federal involvement	National agencies
Cross-border indicators	International coordination	Interpol / border units
Digital activity across regions	Cybercrime jurisdiction	Specialized units
Private investigators	Limited authority	Must defer to police

Pro Tip:

Always confirm jurisdiction formally before initiating searches or data requests.

3. Warrants & Legal Permissions Table

Investigative Action	Legal Requirement	Authorized Party
Search private property	Search warrant	Law enforcement
Access phone / email data	Court order / subpoena	Law enforcement
Seize digital devices	Seizure warrant	Law enforcement
Deploy drones over private land	Airspace + property consent	Operator / Police
Collect DNA / medical records	Court order or consent	Authorized officials
Surveillance / monitoring	Court authorization	Law enforcement

Professional Insight:

Unauthorized actions can invalidate evidence and jeopardize prosecution.

4. Legal Readiness Checklist (Operational)

Task	Responsible Party	Status	Notes / Documentation
File missing person report	Family / Police	☐	Include LKP, photo
Confirm legal classification	Police / Investigator	☐	Missing vs abducted
Verify jurisdiction	Law enforcement	☐	Local / federal
Request warrants if required	Police / Legal counsel	☐	Archive copies
Authorize private investigator	Family	☐	Contract + scope
Log all tips & leads	Family / Investigator	☐	Master Case File
Maintain chain of custody	Investigators	☐	Evidence handling
Review public statements	Communications Officer	☐	Legal compliance
Protect volunteer liability	Search Coordinator	☐	Waivers if needed
Preserve evidence properly	All parties	☐	No contamination

5. Legal Best-Practice Rules

Rule	Why It Matters
Document everything	Creates legal traceability
Respect boundaries	Prevents obstruction charges
Coordinate with police	Avoids jurisdiction conflict
Consult legal counsel	Essential in complex cases
Maintain confidentiality	Protects privacy & strategy

6. Family & Volunteer Legal Guardrails

Action	Allowed	Not Allowed
Public awareness	✔ Approved info only	✘ Speculation
Searching public land	✔ With permission	✘ Trespassing
Collecting tips	✔ Documented	✘ Vigilantism
Media interaction	✔ Via spokesperson	✘ Uncontrolled interviews
Evidence handling	✔ Minimal, documented	✘ Altering scenes

7. Summary — Legal Control Equals Operational Strength

Legal Element	Operational Benefit
Correct classification	Proper priority & resources
Clear jurisdiction	Faster coordination
Warrant compliance	Evidence admissibility
Legal readiness	Reduced chaos
Structured documentation	Case integrity

Core Insight

Law is not an obstacle — it is a force multiplier.

Those who understand it protect the missing person, the searchers, and the truth.

26. Hiring a Private Investigator

Securing Expert Help without Risk

When official resources are constrained or a case requires specialized skills, a licensed private investigator (PI) can accelerate progress. Poor selection, however, introduces legal, financial, and operational risk.

Professional Insight:

A PI augments an investigation — they never replace law enforcement authority.

1. Decision Matrix — When to Hire a Private Investigator

Situation	PI Advantage	Operational Notes
Complex digital footprint	OSINT, cyber-tracing expertise	Must coordinate with police
Interstate / cross-border case	Knowledge of regional law & contacts	Jurisdiction limits apply
Suspected abduction / crime	Professional surveillance & intelligence	Law enforcement alignment required
Case stagnation (48–72 hrs)	Additional manpower & techniques	Vet experience carefully
Sensitive family or media risk	Discreet handling & controlled comms	Avoid publicity-seeking PIs

2. Red-Flag Detection Table — Avoiding Fraud & Liability

Red Flag	Associated Risk	Required Mitigation
Guarantees of results	Impossible, unethical	Reject immediately
Unlicensed / unverifiable	Illegal operations	Verify with regulator
Large upfront payment demand	Financial loss	Use milestone billing
No references or case history	Inexperience	Demand verifiable proof
Vague or secretive methods	Legal exposure	Require methodology outline
Encourages bypassing police	Obstruction risk	Insist on coordination

Rule:

Any PI resisting transparency is a liability, not an asset.

3. Private Investigator Evaluation Scorecard

Use this scorecard to compare candidates objectively.

Evaluation Criteria	Score (1–5)	Verification Notes
Valid license & registration	☐	Regulatory database
Missing-person case experience	☐	Years + case types
Technical capability (OSINT, surveillance)	☐	Tools & methods
References / case studies	☐	Independent verification
Communication clarity & frequency	☐	Reporting samples
Legal & jurisdictional knowledge	☐	Warrants, privacy law
Cost transparency	☐	Written fee schedule
Ethical conduct	☐	No guarantees
Law enforcement coordination	☐	Prior joint cases
Availability / response time	☐	Emergency readiness

Scoring Guide

- **40–50** → Strongly Recommended
- **30–39** → Acceptable with safeguards
- **Below 30** → Do Not Hire

4. Contract Essentials Checklist

Contract Component	Purpose	Status
Scope of work	Defines authority & limits	☐
Confidentiality clause	Protects family & case data	☐
Fee structure	Hourly or milestone-based	☐
Reporting schedule	Written updates defined	☐
Legal compliance clause	Ensures lawful conduct	☐
Evidence handling protocol	Preserves admissibility	☐
Termination clause	Exit without dispute	☐

Best Practice:

No contract = no investigator.

5. Operational Integration Framework

Integration Step	Responsible Party	Control Measure
Introduce PI to command structure	Family / Coordinator	Clear reporting line
Share Master Case File	Coordinator	Verified info only
Assign defined tasks	Coordinator	Avoid duplication
Schedule progress reviews	PI + Coordinator	Weekly minimum
Coordinate with police	PI / Family	Prevent conflicts
Archive all outputs	Documentation Officer	Case integrity

6. Best-Practice Rules (Non-Negotiable)

Rule	Why It Matters
Interview multiple PIs	Prevents impulsive hiring
Verify license independently	Avoids illegal operators
Use written scorecards	Reduces emotional bias
Document all actions	Legal protection
Coordinate with police	Maintains admissibility
Avoid pressure decisions	Scammers exploit urgency

7. Summary — Risk-Controlled Use of Private Investigators

Element	Outcome
Proper vetting	Prevents fraud
Objective scoring	Best candidate selection
Formal contract	Legal protection
Structured integration	Operational efficiency
Police coordination	Evidence validity

Core Insight

The right PI multiplies capability.
The wrong PI multiplies damage.

27. Managing Tips and False Leads

Turning Information Chaos into Actionable Intelligence

In missing-person investigations, most incoming tips are incomplete, duplicated, or incorrect. Without structured control, tips overwhelm investigators and divert resources. A formal lead-management system converts raw information into prioritized, defensible action.

Professional Insight:

Every unverified lead consumes time, manpower, and credibility. Filtering is an operational requirement, not an administrative task.

1. Lead Classification Matrix

Lead Type	Description	Operational Value
Verified	Confirmed by multiple sources or evidence	High – deploy immediately
Plausible	Fits victim profile and timeline, not yet confirmed	Medium – verify quickly
Speculative	Based on rumor, intuition, or social media	Low – monitor only
False / Hoax	Proven incorrect or malicious	None – archive

2. Lead Intake Protocol (Mandatory)

Step	Action	Responsible Party
1	Log lead immediately	Documentation Officer
2	Assign unique lead ID	Documentation Officer
3	Capture full details (who, what, where, when, how)	Intake Officer
4	Assign preliminary category	Investigator / Coordinator
5	Apply scoring & priority	Search Coordinator

Rule: No lead moves forward without a log entry.

3. Lead Filtering Decision Framework

Step	Assessment Question	If YES	If NO
1	Are there verifiable details (time, place, description)?	Proceed to verification	Archive / monitor
2	Does it match the missing person profile?	Elevate priority	Downgrade
3	Is the source credible or identifiable?	Fast-track review	Secondary verification
4	Is the lead time-sensitive (<24 hrs)?	Immediate response	Scheduled review
5	Does it require police authority?	Notify law enforcement	Continue internal checks
6	Is it a duplicate of an existing lead?	Merge records	Assign new ID
7	Verification completed	Mark actionable	Archive

Professional Insight:

Only verified, high-probability leads justify field deployment.

4. Lead Scoring System

Lead Attribute	Score
Verified eyewitness	+5
Direct sighting within 24 hours	+5
Geographic alignment with LKP	+4
Description match	+4
Indirect / secondhand report	+3
Social media source	+2
Anonymous / unverifiable	0

Action Thresholds

Total Score	Required Action
12–15	Immediate deployment
8–11	Rapid verification
≤7	Archive / passive monitoring

5. Operational Lead Management Checklist

Task	Responsible Party	Status	Notes
Log all incoming tips	Documentation Officer	☐	Timestamp required
Assign lead ID & score	Search Coordinator	☐	Use scoring table
Prioritize leads	Investigator	☐	High / Medium / Low
Verify credibility	Investigator / Police	☐	Multi-source check
Track actions taken	Documentation Officer	☐	Who, when, outcome
Update command & family	Coordinator	☐	Controlled briefings
Archive false leads	Documentation Officer	☐	Maintain audit trail

6. Common Pitfalls & Controls

Pitfall	Operational Risk	Control Measure
Acting on rumors	Resource drain	Enforce filtering rules
Volunteer overload	Missed real leads	Deploy only verified tips
Ignoring repeat tips	Missed pattern	Merge duplicates
Emotional bias	Mis-prioritization	Use score thresholds
Public reaction to hoaxes	Legal & media damage	Verify before release

7. Master Case File Integration

Requirement	Standard
Central lead register	Mandatory
Separate verified / unverified tabs	Required
Record verification outcome	Investigator name & date
Link actions taken	Full audit trail
Share with law enforcement	Controlled access

Professional Insight:

Well-managed leads protect investigators from distraction and preserve credibility with law enforcement and media.

8. Summary

Principle	Outcome
Structured intake	Prevents chaos
Objective scoring	Focuses resources
Documentation discipline	Legal defensibility
Rapid action on verified leads	Maximizes recovery probability

Core Truth

Every verified lead is a potential breakthrough.

Every unfiltered rumor is operational waste.

28. Family Survival Guide

Managing Ambiguous Grief & Maintaining Operational Resilience

When a loved one is missing, families experience **ambiguous grief**—a condition defined by uncertainty, lack of closure, and prolonged emotional stress. Without structure, this state degrades judgment, coordination, and long-term resilience.

This chapter provides a **disciplined, checklist-driven framework** to stabilize families emotionally while preserving operational effectiveness.

1. Ambiguous Grief — Impact Assessment Table

Characteristic	**Description**	**Operational Impact**
Lack of closure	No confirmation of outcome	Chronic anxiety, decision paralysis
Conflicting emotions	Hope coexists with despair	Guilt, second-guessing decisions
Disrupted routines	Normal life suspended	Sleep loss, health decline
Emotional volatility	Rapid mood shifts	Family conflict, breakdown in coordination
Social isolation	Feeling misunderstood	Reduced external support
Hyper-vigilance	Constant alert state	Burnout, impaired judgment

Operational Reality:

Ambiguous grief is not weakness—it is a predictable stress response that must be **managed, not ignored**.

2. Core Principles of Family Operational Resilience

Principle	Operational Application
Accept uncertainty	Avoid forcing conclusions or timelines
Create structure	Use schedules, roles, and logs
Regulate emotion	Prevent impulsive decisions
Preserve health	Physical collapse degrades operations
Distribute responsibility	Prevent single-point burnout
Focus on controllables	Restores agency and clarity

3. Family Resilience Framework (Command-Level Table)

Pillar	Required Actions	Implementation Notes
Emotional Awareness	Daily emotional check-ins	Journaling or brief verbal check
Physical Health	Sleep, hydration, nutrition	Non-negotiable baseline
Information Control	Single update coordinator	Prevent rumor overload
Task Engagement	Assign defined roles	Action reduces helplessness
Support Systems	Engage counselor/ support group	Trauma-informed support preferred
Media Exposure Control	Limit news/social intake	Review only verified sources
Decision Discipline	Use scoring & checklists	Avoid emotion-driven choices
Coping Rituals	Daily grounding practice	Stabilizes nervous system

4. Daily Family Resilience Checklist

Task	Responsible Party	Status	Notes
Morning grounding (breathing / meditation)	Assigned family member	☐	5–10 minutes
Health check (sleep, food, medication)	Each individual	☐	Report issues early
Update Master Case File	Documentation Officer	☐	Leads, contacts, actions
Volunteer & task assignment	Coordinator	☐	Prevent overload
Media review (controlled)	Communications Lead	☐	Verify before exposure
Emotional check-in	Family lead / counselor	☐	Identify stress spikes
Evening reflection	Family	☐	Journaling or short discussion

5. Psychological Stress Response Matrix

Stressor	Indicator	Approved Mitigation
Anxiety about outcome	Racing thoughts, insomnia	Breathing, grounding exercises
Emotional exhaustion	Irritability, withdrawal	Rotate responsibilities
Media saturation	Doom scrolling	Time-restricted review
Family conflict	Escalating arguments	Structured debrief, mediator
Loss of control	Despair, paralysis	Assign concrete tasks

6. Professional Support Integration Checklist

Support Type	Purpose	Status
Trauma counselor (ambiguous loss)	Emotional regulation	☐
Peer support group	Shared experience	☐
Volunteer coordinator	Structured engagement	☐
Legal advisor	Reduces uncertainty	☐
Investigative advisor	Maintains clarity	☐

Guidance:

Support is a **force multiplier**, not a sign of failure.

7. Warning Signs of Operational Degradation

Indicator	Required Action
Family member collapse	Immediate role reassignment
Escalating conflict	Pause decisions, mediate
Impulsive decisions	Revert to checklist-based review
Sleep deprivation	Mandatory rest rotation
Obsession with rumors	Information lockdown

8. Command Guidance for Families

- Emotion must be **acknowledged**, not allowed to dictate operations
- Structure protects both **mental health and investigation quality**
- Long searches are **marathons**, not sprints
- Families who remain disciplined become **assets**, not casualties, of the search

Chapter Summary

- Ambiguous grief is **real, prolonged, and destabilizing**
- Structured routines preserve clarity and endurance
- Action-oriented roles restore agency
- Emotional survival is **operational survival**

Core Truth

A family that remains structured under uncertainty becomes the strongest pillar of a sustained search.

29. Resolution, Recovery, and the Unanswered

Navigating Outcomes and Achieving Closure

The resolution phase of a missing-person case is operationally and psychologically decisive. Whether the person is found alive, found deceased, or never located, **unstructured handling at this stage can cause long-term harm**, legal complications, and unresolved trauma.

Professional Insight:

Preparation for all outcomes preserves judgment, protects families, and ensures that closure—when possible—is handled with dignity and discipline.

1. Outcome Pathway: Found Alive — Operational Checklist

Action	Responsible Party	Status	Notes
Secure location & ensure safety	Law enforcement	☐	Prevent secondary harm
Medical evaluation	Emergency medical team	☐	Check dehydration, injury
Psychological assessment	Trauma counselor	☐	Screen for shock / PTSD
Safe transport	Search coordinator	☐	Avoid public exposure
Evidence & statement capture	Investigators	☐	Timeline, contacts, movements
Digital footprint preservation	Investigators	☐	Phone, apps, financial data
Family reunification plan	Social worker / counselor	☐	Gradual, structured
Media containment	Communications Officer	☐	Single statement only
Formal case closure	Law enforcement	☐	Update official records
Post-recovery follow-up	Mental health professionals	☐	Monitor reintegration

Operational Note:

Recovery does **not** end the case. Reintegration is a controlled process, not an emotional rush.

2. Outcome Pathway: Found Deceased — Protocol Checklist

Action	Responsible Party	Status	Notes
Secure discovery site	Law enforcement	☐	Preserve evidence
Suspend civilian activity	Search coordinator	☐	Prevent contamination
Family notification (in person)	Police + crisis counselor	☐	Never by media
Post-mortem examination	Medical examiner	☐	Cause & manner of death
Evidence & property handling	Investigators	☐	Chain of custody
Legal case update	Law enforcement / legal counsel	☐	Close or reclassify
Media statement control	Communications Officer	☐	Factual, minimal
Family grief support	Counselors / support groups	☐	Immediate + long-term
Volunteer transition	Search coordinator	☐	From search to support
Memorial & closure planning	Family support lead	☐	Optional, family-led

Professional Insight:

How death is handled often determines whether families heal—or remain trapped in trauma.

3. Outcome Pathway: Never Found — Long-Term Management Checklist

Action	Responsible Party	Status	Notes
Maintain Master Case File	Family / investigator	☐	Central intelligence archive
Define case status	Law enforcement	☐	Active / inactive / cold
Schedule periodic reviews	Investigator	☐	Technology & lead refresh
Preserve evidence legally	Investigators	☐	Long-term integrity
Media strategy (controlled)	Communications Officer	☐	Prevent rumor cycles
Ongoing mental health care	Counselors	☐	Ambiguous grief focus
Peer support engagement	Family	☐	Prevent isolation
Anniversary protocol	Family / counselor	☐	Emotional risk periods
Contingency planning	Family lead	☐	If new lead emerges

Operational Reality:

Unresolved does **not** mean unmanaged. Structure prevents emotional collapse.

4. Closure Pathways Framework (Comparative Table)

Outcome	Psychological Focus	Operational Focus	Family Support Priority
Found Alive	Reintegration, safety	Debrief, rehab, documentation	Therapy, gradual reunification
Found Deceased	Grief, mourning	Evidence handling, legal closure	Trauma counseling, memorial
Never Found	Ambiguous loss	Case maintenance, review cycles	Long-term support, acceptance tools

5. Post-Resolution Governance Rules

Rule	Purpose
Document everything	Legal, insurance, historical record
Formalize closure status	Prevent confusion or false hope
Maintain counseling routines	Trauma persists after outcome
Control narrative	Protect dignity & privacy
Preserve case materials	Future breakthroughs possible
Acknowledge volunteers	Ethical and community closure

6. Warning Signs after Resolution

Indicator	Required Response
Sudden emotional collapse	Immediate counseling
Obsessive case re-investigation	Re-establish boundaries
Family conflict escalation	Mediated intervention
Media fixation	Communication lockdown
Withdrawal from support	Re-engage network

7. Final Takeaways

- Resolution is **not an endpoint**, but a transition
- Each outcome demands **different protocols**
- Closure requires **both procedure and care**
- Structure protects families long after searches end

Core Truth

Closure is not only about answers —
it is about how people are carried through what comes next.

30. Advanced Behavioral Analytics

Predicting Movement, Understanding Risk, and Acting before a Crisis

Purpose

Behavioral analytics is the systematic study of human behavior to identify patterns, assess risk, and anticipate actions before they escalate into disappearance, abduction, or criminal harm. This chapter provides **structured tools** for families, investigators, and journalists to convert behavioral observations into **measurable risk intelligence** and **early intervention strategies.**

Professional Insight

Disappearances are rarely spontaneous. Behavioral deviations, environmental stressors, and decision-making shifts often emerge **days to months** beforehand. Early recognition enables prevention, faster response, and higher recovery probability.

1. Foundations of Behavioral Analysis

Concept	Description	Operational Application
Pre-Disappearance Indicators	Emotional, behavioral, or social signals preceding disappearance	Early risk identification and preventive intervention
Pattern Recognition	Recurring routines, movements, contacts, or digital behavior	Predicts likely locations, timing, and movement
Cognitive Profiling	Personality traits, stress response, decision-making tendencies	Guides interviews, search priorities, and communication strategy
Environmental Factors	Work, relationships, finances, digital exposure, threats	Adjusts overall risk score and probability models
Behavioral Deviations	Noticeable breaks from established routines or habits	High-alert triggers for escalation protocols

2. Predictive Behavioral Assessment Flow (Checklist-Based)

Step 1: Initial Behavioral Observation

Indicator Present?	Yes	No
Sudden withdrawal or isolation	☐	☐
Mood instability or emotional shifts	☐	☐
Unusual communication patterns	☐	☐
Secretive behavior or unexplained movements	☐	☐

If YES to any → Proceed to Step 2

If NO → Continue routine monitoring

Step 2: Risk Factor Scoring Checklist

Risk Factor	Score
Minor or vulnerable individual in high-risk environment	+3
Adult experiencing financial, legal, or personal crisis	+2
Recent threats, harassment, coercion, or stalking	+4
Mental health warning signs or destabilization	+2

Step 3: Probability Assessment

Total Score	Risk Level	Required Action
≥ 7	**High Priority**	Immediate escalation and intervention
4–6	**Moderate Alert**	Targeted monitoring and data collection
≤ 3	**Low Risk**	Routine documentation and check-ins

Step 4: Action Pathways

Risk Level	Operational Response
High	Notify authorities, preserve digital evidence, activate surveillance and safety planning
Moderate	Interview contacts, analyze digital footprint, track movements
Low	Maintain behavior logs, periodic review

3. Red-Flag Monitoring Dashboard (Daily Use)

Signal	Category	Risk Level	Required Action
Frequent unexplained absences	Behavioral	Medium	Interview, document, monitor
Sudden asset liquidation	Financial	High	Investigate financial records
Withdrawal from social circles	Social	Medium	Contact associates, assess isolation
Digital behavior anomalies	Digital	High	OSINT review, device analysis
Threats or harassment history	Environmental	High	Notify authorities, safety plan
Substance misuse or erratic behavior	Behavioral	Medium	Monitor, recommend support
Repeated exposure to risky locations	Environmental	Medium	Track routes and map activity

Operational Note: Review this dashboard **daily** and update the Master Case File accordingly.

4. Behavioral Probability Scoring Template

Factor	Observation	Weight	Score	Notes
Social withdrawal		2		
Financial instability		3		
Threats or coercion		4		
Online activity anomalies		3		
Mental health warning signs		2		
Travel or disappearance pattern		4		

Total Score: ______

Assigned Risk Level: Low ☐ / Moderate ☐ / High ☐

5. Operational Strategies Using Behavioral Analytics

Behavioral Intelligence Checklist

Task	Completed
Daily behavioral logging maintained	☐
Routine vs deviation patterns identified	☐
Digital behavior reviewed	☐
Social and environmental stressors assessed	☐
Risk score recalculated	☐

Integration Protocols

Strategy	Purpose
Risk Matrix Integration	Combine behavioral scores with threat analysis (see Chapter 3)
Scenario Simulation	Model likely movements and destinations
Cross-Referencing	Align with LKP data (Chapter 4) and OSINT findings (Chapter 20)
Alert Thresholds	Define score-based escalation to authorities
Training Distribution	Educate families and teams on behavior logging

6. Key Takeaways

- Behavioral signals precede most disappearances.
- Structured scoring replaces intuition with actionable intelligence.

- Early intervention significantly increases recovery outcomes.
- Behavioral analytics bridges **observation → prediction → response.**

Core Truth

The missing often signal their risk through subtle behavioral shifts. Those who recognize and act on these signals move from reaction to prevention.

31. Real-Case Global Breakdowns

Learning from International Missing-Person Investigations

Purpose

Real-world cases translate theory into operational reality. By examining **successful recoveries, investigative failures, and unresolved disappearances** across countries and cultures, this chapter identifies **repeatable best practices**, common pitfalls, and decision points that materially affect outcomes.

Professional Insight

Frameworks only become reliable when tested against reality. Studying real cases equips investigators and families to anticipate obstacles, deploy resources efficiently, and avoid preventable delays.

1. Standardized Case Study Framework

Use the following format for **every case review** to enable cross-case comparison and pattern identification.

Attribute	Description
Region / Country	Geographic and jurisdictional context
Missing Person Profile	Age, gender, occupation, vulnerabilities, risk factors
Circumstances of Disappearance	Location, time, activity, situational context
Initial Response	Family actions, reporting timeline, early errors
Investigative Tools Used	OSINT, behavioral analytics, surveillance, field search
Key Decisions & Strategies	Actions that accelerated or obstructed progress
Outcome	Recovered alive, deceased, unresolved
Lessons Learned	Practical, transferable insights

Operational Note: Consistent documentation enables trend analysis across borders and case types.

2. Sample Global Case Breakdowns

Case 1: Child Abduction — Urban United States

Attribute	Details
Region	New York City, USA
Missing Person Profile	10-year-old boy, student
Circumstances	Last seen at neighborhood playground after school
Initial Response	Police notification delayed by 2 hours; uncoordinated family search
Investigative Tools Used	CCTV triage, neighborhood canvassing, social media alerts
Key Decisions & Strategies	Rapid CCTV prioritization narrowed suspect pool within 12 hours
Outcome	Found alive in abandoned building after 18 hours
Lessons Learned	Golden Hour Protocol is critical; structured social media alerts increase tip quality

Case 2: Teen Runaway — Rural India

Attribute	Details
Region	Maharashtra, India
Missing Person Profile	16-year-old female, recent family conflict
Circumstances	Left home at night; phone switched off
Initial Response	Family-led village search; police notified after 24 hours
Investigative Tools Used	Behavioral profiling, LKP mapping, community interviews
Key Decisions & Strategies	Probability-ring search focused volunteer efforts
Outcome	Located after 3 days at a city hostel (voluntary absence)
Lessons Learned	Behavioral analytics distinguish runaway vs abduction early

Case 3: Adult Voluntary Disappearance — United Kingdom

Attribute	Details
Region	London, UK
Missing Person Profile	35-year-old male, financial and emotional stress
Circumstances	Left job and residence; ceased contact
Initial Response	Family panic; fragmented, uncoordinated search
Investigative Tools Used	Digital footprint analysis, banking records, ride-share data
Key Decisions & Strategies	OSINT triangulation reduced search radius within 48 hours
Outcome	Found alive; preparing relocation
Lessons Learned	Digital intelligence is decisive in adult voluntary cases

Case 4: International Child Abduction — Cross-Border Europe

Attribute	Details
Region	France → Germany
Missing Person Profile	8-year-old girl
Circumstances	Abducted from public park
Initial Response	Immediate reporting; early jurisdictional confusion
Investigative Tools Used	INTERPOL alerts, OSINT, LKP mapping, cross-border coordination
Key Decisions & Strategies	Unified international command accelerated information flow
Outcome	Rescued alive within 36 hours
Lessons Learned	Jurisdiction clarity and global networks save time and lives

3. Cross-Case Operational Insights

Insight	Practical Application
Early reporting reduces search time	Apply Golden Hour Protocol (Chapter 2)
Behavioral + digital data increases prediction accuracy	Chapters 3, 10, 31
Clear command structure prevents search chaos	Chapters 21–23
Cross-border coordination is decisive	Chapter 26 + Extra Chapter 5
Tip verification preserves resources	Chapter 28
Family resilience sustains long operations	Chapter 29

4. Case Review Checklist (For Training & Analysis)

Task	Completed
Case documented using standardized template	☐
Initial response timeline evaluated	☐
Investigative tools assessed for effectiveness	☐
Decision points analyzed	☐
Errors and delays identified	☐
Transferable lessons extracted	☐
Findings added to Master Case Reference	☐

5. Key Takeaways

- Real cases expose **recurring failure points**: delayed reporting, misinformation, and poor coordination.
- The frameworks in this guide—**risk scoring, LKP, behavioral analytics, digital tracking**—are validated by real-world success.
- Structured documentation and global collaboration significantly improve outcomes.
- While every case is unique, **operational discipline and verification principles are universal**.

Professional Insight

Studying real cases converts knowledge into foresight. Each breakdown strengthens decision-making, sharpens judgment, and prepares responders for the realities they will face.

32. Decision Trees & Crisis Algorithms

Structured Choices for Rapid, High-Stakes Response

Purpose

Missing-person investigations unfold under intense time pressure, emotional strain, and incomplete information. Decision trees and crisis algorithms provide **pre-mapped logic paths** that reduce hesitation, prevent resource misallocation, and enable decisive action—especially during the **Golden Hour** and early escalation phases.

Professional Insight

In high-stakes searches, uncertainty is inevitable. Indecision is optional. Predefined decision structures transform chaos into coordinated response.

1. Golden Hour Decision Tree (0–24 Hours)

Use this table sequentially. Each step informs the next action.

Step	Decision Question	Action if YES	Action if NO
1	Is the disappearance confirmed (not a delay)?	Activate immediate response	Continue short-term monitoring
2	Is the person a child or high-risk adult?	Notify law enforcement immediately	Issue standard alert
3	Are digital devices accessible?	Secure phone, computer, accounts	Proceed to physical search
4	Last seen in a public location?	Request CCTV and witnesses	Focus on private/ residential leads
5	Suspicious factors present (threats, coercion)?	Escalate as possible abduction	Treat as voluntary/ runaway
6	Witnesses or leads available?	Interview and log immediately	Record for later verification
7	Time elapsed >12 hours?	Expand search radius	Maintain LKP-focused search

Operational Tip: Run this decision tree alongside the **Master Case File** (Chapter 5) and **Risk Scoring Matrix** (Chapter 3).

2. Lead Prioritization Algorithm (Tips & Information Control)

This algorithm prevents resource drain caused by false or low-quality tips.

Step	Evaluation Question	Action if YES	Action if NO
1	Is the tip verifiable?	Proceed to verification	Archive and monitor
2	Matches LKP & probability models?	Assign field/digital resources	Deprioritize
3	Source credibility high?	Immediate follow-up	Cross-check sources
4	Time-sensitive (<24h)?	Rapid deployment	Schedule review
5	Legal or jurisdictional impact?	Notify authorities	Continue independent review
6	Lead score ≥ threshold (e.g., ≥12)?	Allocate resources	Log and archive

Professional Insight: Pair this algorithm with numerical lead scoring to avoid emotional bias (see Chapter 28).

3. Risk Escalation Pathway

This pathway ensures **proportional response** and avoids overreaction or under-response.

Trigger Event	Risk Level	Immediate Action	Follow-Up
Verified high-probability lead	High	Deploy search; notify police	Update Master Case File
Abduction indicators	Critical	Escalate to higher authorities	Activate media & OSINT
Threats or coercion detected	High	Secure family; preserve evidence	Monitor communications
Disappearance >24 hours	Medium	Expand search radius	Reassess analytics
Conflicting or false leads	Low	Archive and monitor	Re-evaluate if new data

4. Crisis Simulation Algorithm (72-Hour Operational Plan)

Use this as a **baseline action model** adaptable to case specifics.

Timeframe	Action	Responsible Party	Notes
0–1 hr	Confirm disappearance; contact authorities	Family / Documentation Officer	Use Golden Hour protocol
1–4 hrs	Establish LKP; secure digital data	Investigator / Family	Devices, accounts, logs
4–8 hrs	Interview close contacts and neighbors	Lead Investigator	Document all statements
8–12 hrs	Deploy field search or volunteers	Search Coordinator	Grid, line, spiral methods
12–24 hrs	Expand search; media alerts if needed	Coordinator / Media Officer	OSINT integration
24–48 hrs	Behavioral, financial, digital analysis	Forensics / OSINT Team	Cross-reference leads
48–72 hrs	Reassess risk; reprioritize leads	Master Case File Team	Update decision paths

Professional Insight: Continuous action cycles prevent operational stagnation and decision fatigue.

5. Crisis Decision-Making Checklist

Use during active operations to maintain discipline.

Task	Completed
Golden Hour decision tree executed	☐
Lead prioritization algorithm applied	☐
Risk escalation level assigned	☐
Command roles clearly defined	☐
Documentation updated in real time	☐
Decision paths reviewed every 12–24 hrs	☐

6. Key Takeaways

- Decision trees convert emotional pressure into structured action.
- Algorithms reduce bias and prevent wasted effort.
- Risk escalation ensures the right response at the right time.
- Unified frameworks allow families, volunteers, and investigators to operate cohesively.

Core Truth

In missing-person investigations, structure outperforms instinct. Imperfect action guided by a clear decision framework saves more lives than hesitation driven by fear of error.

33. Tech-Integrated Investigation Toolkit

Harnessing AI, Drones, and Digital Intelligence in Missing-Person Cases

Purpose

Technology now plays a decisive role in missing-person investigations by accelerating discovery, expanding search reach, and improving predictive accuracy. This chapter provides a **modular, legally conscious toolkit** enabling families, investigators, and trained volunteers to integrate digital intelligence, aerial assets, and AI-assisted analysis into coordinated operations—without requiring advanced technical expertise.

Professional Insight

Technology does not replace investigators—it multiplies their effectiveness. When used correctly, it shortens timelines, clarifies uncertainty, and saves lives.

1. Digital Footprint Mapping

Digital behavior often provides the **earliest and most reliable clues** in modern disappearances.

Tool / Method	**Purpose**	**Operational Notes**
Social Media Monitoring	Identify last interactions, locations, behavioral changes	Aggregate Facebook, Instagram, TikTok, WhatsApp, X
Cloud Account Metadata	Access login times, IP locations, device history	Obtain consent or legal authority
Ride-Share & Transport Logs	Track movements via taxis, buses, rideshare	Cross-reference with LKP and timelines
Financial Transactions	Detect withdrawals, purchases, or anomalies	Integrate with Financial Forensics (Chapter 17)
Device Triangulation	Estimate movement via cell towers & GPS	Build probability rings

Professional Tip: Preserve all digital evidence with timestamps and access logs to maintain admissibility if the case escalates legally.

2. Drone & Aerial Reconnaissance Operations

Aerial assets dramatically reduce search time and risk to human searchers.

Capability	Use Case	Operational Considerations
Quadcopters / Fixed-Wing Drones	Wilderness, rooftops, inaccessible terrain	Confirm airspace rules, battery logistics
Thermal Imaging	Night searches, foliage, water edges	Most effective within first 72 hours
Real-Time Video Feed	Ground-air coordination	Assign trained operator
Geotagged Imaging	GPS-linked imagery	Upload to Master Case File

Professional Insight

Drones convert hours of ground searching into minutes of aerial intelligence, especially in low-visibility or hazardous terrain.

3. AI-Powered Search & Pattern Recognition

AI tools increase **speed and scale**, but require **human oversight** to avoid false positives.

Technology	Purpose	Practical Application
Facial Recognition AI	Identify missing persons in CCTV or public media	Rapid scanning of large footage datasets
Predictive Analytics	Anticipate movement based on behavior	Combine with LKP & risk scoring
Geospatial AI	Model likely routes & destinations	Incorporate terrain & transport data
OSINT AI Monitoring	Track forums, chats, social platforms	Early detection of abduction or voluntary flight
Data Fusion Platforms	Merge all intelligence sources	Unified operational dashboard

Professional Tip: AI identifies patterns—humans confirm truth.

4. Geospatial & Mapping Tools

Visual intelligence improves coordination and prevents duplication.

Tool	Purpose	Notes
GIS Mapping Software	Visualize search zones & probability rings	Overlay roads, terrain, waterways
Heat Maps	Identify high-probability locations	Update dynamically
Volunteer Deployment Maps	Assign search sectors	Sync with aerial & AI outputs

Professional Insight

Mapping tools turn scattered data into shared situational awareness, aligning all teams around the same operational picture.

5. Operational Integration Checklist

Use this checklist to ensure **coordinated execution** across all technical assets.

Step	Task	Responsible	Status
1	Secure devices for digital analysis	Family / Investigator	☐
2	Upload LKP & risk matrix into GIS	Investigator	☐
3	Deploy drones / aerial units	Field Coordinator	☐
4	Activate AI & OSINT tools	Digital Analyst	☐
5	Assign mapped zones to volunteers	Search Coordinator	☐
6	Fuse data from all sources	Lead Investigator	☐
7	Monitor & update in real time	All Teams	☐

Professional Insight

Maximum effectiveness occurs when human searchers, digital intelligence, and aerial assets operate as one system.

6. Ethical & Legal Safeguards

Technology must be used responsibly to protect rights and ensure admissibility.

Principle	Requirement
Privacy Compliance	Follow local and international data-protection laws
Airspace Regulations	Observe drone permits and flight restrictions
AI Oversight	Require human confirmation for all AI-generated leads
Evidence Preservation	Maintain audit trails, logs, and timestamps

Core Truth

Technology accelerates discovery—but only disciplined, ethical use transforms speed into success.

7. Key Takeaways

- Technology shifts investigations from reactive to predictive.
- AI, drones, GIS, and OSINT dramatically expand reach and efficiency.
- Integration, verification, and legality are as important as innovation.
- Families and investigators using this toolkit gain decisive advantage—especially within the **Golden Hour** and **first 72 hours**.

Professional Insight

Technology does not find the missing by itself. It is the **coordinated partnership between people and tools** that brings them home.

34. Global Resource & Network Blueprint

Connecting Families, Investigators, and Agencies Across Borders

Purpose

Missing-person cases frequently cross borders—physically, digitally, or jurisdictionally. Delays often occur not because of lack of effort, but because **contacts, protocols, and escalation paths are unclear at the moment they are needed.**

This chapter provides a **pre-mapped, actionable global network framework** enabling families, investigators, and coordinators to activate the right resources **immediately**, locally and internationally.

Professional Insight

In cross-border cases, preparedness is leverage. Knowing *who* to contact, *when*, and *how* can save critical hours—or lives.

1. International Law Enforcement & Multinational Agencies

Organization	Scope	Primary Application	Operational Notes
INTERPOL – Yellow Notices	Global	Cross-border missing persons & child abduction	Requires national law enforcement submission
FBI – Missing Persons / AMBER Alert	United States	Federal coordination, digital & field support	AMBER limited to qualifying child cases
Europol – Missing Persons Unit	Europe	Multi-country intelligence sharing	Supports EU member states
Red Cross – Restoring Family Links	Global humanitarian	Voluntary disappearances, disaster separation	Neutral, non-law-enforcement role
UNICEF – Child Protection	Global	Child trafficking & protection	Focus on prevention and recovery

Professional Tip: Pre-identify **points of contact** within these agencies before a crisis occurs.

2. National & Federal Agencies (Sample Framework)

Use this structure to build **country-specific directories.**

Country / Region	Key Agency	Specialization	Notes
India	National Crime Records Bureau (NCRB)	Missing children & adults	Centralized national data
United Kingdom	National Crime Agency (NCA)	High-risk adult & abduction cases	Strong international links
United States	NCMEC	Missing & exploited children	Digital forensics & OSINT
Canada	RCMP – Missing Persons	Adult & child cases	Federal jurisdiction
Australia	Australian Federal Police	High-risk cases	INTERPOL coordination

Operational Note: Always confirm **local escalation thresholds** and reporting timelines.

3. NGO & Civilian Support Networks

NGOs and civilian networks **extend reach, manpower, and visibility** beyond official channels.

Network	Focus Area	Operational Value
Missing Children Europe	Child safety & tracing	Regional alerts & databases
International Child Rescue	Abduction & trafficking	Rapid response & awareness
Global Search & Rescue Volunteer Networks	Field search operations	Manpower & terrain access
Social Media Crowdsourcing Platforms	Public awareness & tips	Speed and reach

Professional Insight: NGOs supplement—not replace—law enforcement. Coordination is essential to avoid duplication or misinformation.

4. Cross-Border Collaboration Checklist (Operational Template)

Step	Task	Responsible Role	Notes
1	Confirm jurisdiction & authority	Lead Investigator	Identify primary & secondary jurisdictions
2	Notify relevant international agencies	Investigator / Family	Use standardized notice templates
3	Activate NGOs & volunteer networks	Search Coordinator	Provide LKP & probability maps
4	Share OSINT & digital footprint data	Digital Analyst	Use secure, encrypted channels
5	Coordinate multi-jurisdiction field searches	Field Coordinator	Single command structure
6	Log all communications	Documentation Officer	Legal & operational traceability
7	Update Master Case File	Investigator	Integrate with analytics & risk scoring

Professional Insight

The difference between speed and delay is often documentation prepared *before* it is needed.

5. Resource Directory Template (Maintain Locally)

Families and investigators should maintain a **living directory** like the example below.

Category	Resource Name	Contact	Notes
Law Enforcement	INTERPOL Yellow Notice	National police channel	Cross-border cases
NGO	Red Cross – Restoring Family Links	Regional chapter	Humanitarian tracing
Tech / OSINT	Crisis AI Platforms	Platform-specific	Pattern detection
Volunteer Network	Global Search & Rescue	Regional coordinator	Field operations
Legal Support	International Human Rights Firms	Varies by country	Jurisdictional advice

6. Integration with Other Frameworks

Chapter	Integration Point
Chapter 3	Risk scoring informs escalation
Chapter 5	Master Case File centralizes contacts
Chapter 26	Cross-jurisdiction coordination
Chapter 31	Behavioral analytics refine scope
Chapter 33	Decision trees trigger agency activation
Chapter 34	Tech tools support global data sharing

7. Key Takeaways

- Pre-mapped networks eliminate critical delays.
- Cross-border investigations require **legal clarity and secure**

communication.

- NGOs and volunteers amplify—but must be coordinated with—official efforts.
- Even voluntary disappearances benefit from structured global contact mapping.
- Network strength directly impacts speed, reach, and outcomes.

Core Truth

Missing-person investigations are no longer local problems. The faster and stronger your global network, the higher the probability of resolution.

Bonus Sections

Elite Tier Operational Tools

Advanced Assets for High-Risk, Time-Critical Missing-Person Operations

1. The 72-Hour War Plan

Critical-Phase Operational Blueprint (Hour-by-Hour)

The first 72 hours determine trajectory, probability, and outcome. This plan assigns **clear tasks, ownership, and tools** for every phase.

Hour	Task	Responsible	Notes / Tools
0–1	Confirm disappearance; establish Last Known Point (LKP)	Family / Lead Investigator	Golden Hour Template (Ch. 2)
1–4	Notify law enforcement & relevant cross-border agencies	Lead Investigator	Local Police / INTERPOL
4–8	Secure digital devices, social accounts, cloud access	Digital Analyst	OSINT Toolkit (Ch. 20)
8–12	Conduct priority interviews (family, friends, neighbors)	Interview Team	Question Bank (Ch. 9)
12–24	Deploy field search (grid / linear / spiral)	Field Coordinator	Volunteer Maps (Ch. 21)
24–36	Expand search; integrate drones & aerial assets	Tech / Drone Team	Drone Matrix (Ch. 22)
36–48	Behavioral, financial & digital analysis	Behavioral / Forensics	Risk Scoring (Ch. 3)
48–60	Verify leads, filter false tips, escalate credible ones	Lead Investigator	Tip Algorithm (Ch. 28)
60–72	Review progress; update decision trees; plan next phase	Master Case File Team	Crisis Algorithms (Ch. 33)

Key Takeaways

- Every hour has **purpose, ownership, and tools**
- Prevents downtime, duplication, and decision paralysis
- Integrates Golden Hour, LKP, Behavioral Analytics, OSINT, and Field Operations into **one synchronized plan**

2. Missing Child Emergency Card

Pocket-Size Rapid-Response Reference

Designed for **immediate handoff** to law enforcement, schools, neighbors, and responders.

Section	Content
Child Information	Name, age, recent photo, physical description, distinguishing marks
Last Seen	Date, time, location, witnesses
Immediate Action	Police number, local agency, child helpline
Digital Identifiers	Phone number, social media handles, email
Escalation Contacts	National & cross-border agency details
Notes	Sightings, behavior changes, updates

Operational Tip

Families should **carry multiple copies**, keep a **digital scan**, and provide one to schools, caregivers, and local authorities *before* an incident occurs.

3. Investigator's Field Notebook

Structured Documentation for Accuracy & Legal Integrity

Section	Purpose
Daily Log	Time-stamped actions, movements, and decisions
Witness Statements	Names, contacts, summaries, verification status
Field Evidence	Photos, GPS coordinates, descriptions, chain-of-custody
Volunteer Deployment	Team assignments, zones, shift outcomes
Digital Evidence	Screenshots, device logs, metadata
Case Status	Verified leads, pending leads, next actions

Professional Insight

Meticulous field notes protect **case integrity**, strengthen **legal admissibility**, and enable **future review or escalation**.

4. Psychological Stability Guide for Families

Emotional Resilience as an Operational Asset

Aspect	Operational Guidance
Ambiguous Grief	Structured check-ins, journaling, counseling
Stress Regulation	Breathing drills, short routines, grounding exercises
Communication	Central update channel; single point-of-contact
Support Network	Friends, NGOs, community leaders
Volunteer Interaction	Assign liaison to prevent overload
Decision-Making	Use checklists & decision trees to reduce panic

Core Insight

Emotional stability is not optional—it directly improves coordination, memory accuracy, and decision quality.

5. National & International Resource Directory

Rapid Access to Global Support

Category	Organization	Scope / Use
Law Enforcement	INTERPOL – Yellow Notices	Cross-border alerts
Law Enforcement	FBI / NCMEC (USA)	Child & adult cases
NGOs	Red Cross – Restoring Family Links	Humanitarian tracing
Volunteer Networks	Global Search & Rescue	Field deployment
Digital / Tech	Crisis AI & OSINT Platforms	Predictive analytics
Legal	International Human Rights Law Firms	Cross-border legal aid
Media	Investigative Journalism Networks	Public awareness & tips

Blueprint for Agencies

Network Maintenance & Readiness

Task	Responsible	Frequency	Notes
Update global & national contacts	Admin Officer	Monthly	Verify phone/email/web
Audit OSINT & AI tools	Digital Team	Weekly	Accuracy & legality
Volunteer drills & mapping exercises	Field Coordinator	Quarterly	Test terrain & drones
Review crisis & 72-hr plans	Lead Investigator	Post-case	Integrate lessons learned
Psychological briefing for families	Family Liaison	As needed	Prevent burnout

Final Operational Truth

Elite outcomes are never improvised. They are built from preparation, structure, and disciplined execution under pressure.

Conclusion — From Chaos to Clarity

Navigating a missing-person case is a journey through uncertainty, fear, and emotional turmoil. This book has guided readers step by step—from the **critical first hours**, through **structured searches, investigative frameworks, digital intelligence, and psychological resilience**, to the **complex realities of closure and recovery**.

Key Insight

A missing-person investigation is not solely about locating someone physically. It encompasses **legal, operational, psychological, and social challenges**. Families, investigators, and volunteers are most effective when equipped with **knowledge, structured processes, and emotional resilience**.

This 360° Blueprint Empowers You To:

- Act decisively during the **Golden Hour** and the first 72 hours.
- Apply professional **search techniques** and leverage **digital intelligence tools.**
- Engage **law enforcement, NGOs, and investigative journalists** strategically and legally.
- Manage tips, leads, and misinformation with precision.
- Maintain **family well-being, mental resilience, and emotional clarity** under stress.
- Prepare for all possible outcomes—**found alive, found deceased, or unresolved**—with dignity and operational structure.

By combining **operational expertise, legal knowledge, psychological insight, and field-tested checklists**, this book serves as a **definitive guide** for anyone facing the terrifying unknown of a disappearance. It transforms **chaos into clarity**, **helplessness into action**, and **grief into structured resilience**.

Final Thought

No manual can guarantee a specific outcome, but **preparation, knowledge, and collaboration** maximize the chances of success—and preserve hope when hope feels most fragile.

About the Author — Fazal Abubakkar Esaf

Fazal Abubakkar Esaf is an investigative strategist, researcher, and author with **decades of experience** in missing-person cases, crisis response, and intelligence-led investigations. He has worked closely with **families, law enforcement agencies, private investigators, and media organizations**, bridging the gap between operational procedures and real-world application.

Fazal's work is defined by **approach**: combining **strategic planning, technological tools, legal awareness, and psychological insight** to create actionable frameworks that empower both families and investigators.

Beyond investigations, Fazal is committed to:

- **Advancing public understanding** of crisis response.
- **Promoting mental resilience** for families in distress.
- **Developing practical, global-reference guides** for complex cases.

His publications are recognized for **clarity, operational depth, and empathetic approach**, making complex investigative strategies accessible to professionals and non-specialists alike.

"In the darkest hours of uncertainty, knowledge and preparation are the lights that guide families and investigators to hope, clarity, and resolution." — Fazal Abubakkar Esaf

Don't miss out!

Visit the website below and you can sign up to receive emails whenever faz publishes a new book. There's no charge and no obligation.

https://books2read.com/r/B-A-HEHOD-JZAAJ

BOOKS 2 READ

Connecting independent readers to independent writers.

Did you love *The Disappeared*? Then you should read *Evidence Doesn't Always Cast Shadows*[1] by Fazal Abubakkar Esaf!

[2]

Mystery is everywhere — hidden in silent corridors, behind locked doors, and in the subtle gestures of everyday life.

Suspense is not merely about crime — it thrives in the unnoticed, the overlooked, and the quietly uncanny.

Within these pages, you will encounter vanished guests, murdered artists, cursed theaters, frozen lakes, haunted lighthouses, and clues that defy logic. Each story challenges perception, explores human psychology, and teases the imagination.

Listen to the whispers, notice the glances, and follow the footsteps. Every shadow may conceal a secret. Every silence may hold a story.

---

1. https://books2read.com/u/boR7k0

2. https://books2read.com/u/boR7k0

Welcome to *Evidence Doesn't Always Cast Shadows*, a world where the incomplete, the mysterious, and the unknown come vividly to life.

Also by faz

Unreliable Memories, Quiet Devastations
Ten Percent Human
The Disappeared

www.ingramcontent.com/pod-product-compliance
Lightning Source LLC
LaVergne TN
LVHW090317210926
848480LV00001B/280